LIFE'S OPERATING MANUAL

✳

With the Fear and Truth Dialogues

LIFE'S OPERATING MANUAL

---※---

With the Fear and Truth Dialogues

TOM SHADYAC

HAY HOUSE, INC.
Carlsbad, California • New York City
London • Sydney • Johannesburg
Vancouver • Hong Kong • New Delhi

Published and distributed in the United States by: Hay House, Inc.: www.hayhouse.com • *Published and distributed in Australia by:* Hay House Australia Pty. Ltd.: www.hayhouse.com.au • *Published and distributed in the United Kingdom by:* Hay House UK, Ltd.: www.hayhouse.co.uk • *Published and distributed in the Republic of South Africa by:* Hay House SA (Pty), Ltd.: www.hayhouse.co.za • *Distributed in Canada by:* Raincoast: www.raincoast.com • *Published in India by:* Hay House Publishers India: www.hayhouse.co.in

Cover and interior design: Nita Ybarra

Cataloging-in-Publication Data is on File at the Library of Congress

Hardcover ISBN: 978-1-4019-4309-7

16 15 14 13   5 4 3 2
1st edition, May 2013
2nd edition, May 2013

Printed in the United States of America

Don't think of him as a seeker . . .
Whatever he's looking for, he is that himself.

—RUMI

PREFACE

✳

Don't die . . .
With that holy ruby mine inside
Still unclaimed.

—HAFIZ

I'M A STORYTELLER, a film director for over 25 years, so let me begin with a story . . . In June of 1998, after wrapping *Liar, Liar,* Jim Carrey, another friend, and I decided to head to Alaska to breathe some clean air, revel in nature's beauty, and talk about life, love, and the meaning of it all. A few days into our adventure, we were flying high over the Chugach Mountains when our bush pilot received radio instructions that he needed to deliver gasoline to some 20 hikers stranded on a nearby glacier. That's when the idea hit me: *"Hey, Jim. Why don't you make the delivery?"* In a split second, Jim realized the hilarious potential of this scenario. You see, where we were was beyond remote. Our lodge, for example, was 200 miles from a paved road. You're lucky to see anyone, much less Ace Ventura delivering gasoline. But that's what was about to happen, and when our pilot agreed, we were giddy with anticipation.

It wasn't long before we landed 75 yards or so from the hikers. Jim got out, and with gas can in hand, walked toward the unsuspecting group. He then held the red can high and in Ace Ventura's voice announced, *"Hi, I'm Jim Carrey! I heard you needed some gas!"* I'll never forget those 20 hikers' mouths opening wide in utter disbelief. Jim set the can down, then added: *"Tom Cruise will be by later with some trail mix!"* With dramatic flair, he spun on his heels and headed back to the plane. And with that, we were off, howling with laughter at those flabbergasted faces all frozen with the same expression that said: *Jim Carrey was the last person anyone expected to deliver gas on a glacier in the Alaskan wilderness!*

As I write this, I feel a bit like I'm Jim, and you, perhaps, are the unsuspecting hikers: I'm the last person you might expect to deliver a message about fixing a world gone wrong. I am, after all, in the eyes of that world, just a comedy director—*Ace Ventura: Pet Detective; The Nutty Professor; Liar, Liar; Patch Adams; Bruce Almighty; Evan Almighty*—which makes me an unlikely source for the content of this book. So unlikely, it took a near-death experience to give me the courage to share my story, first in the documentary *I AM,* and now here.

My brush with death was not exactly the stuff of legend or even worthy of a Hallmark movie. It was a routine concussion from a mountain bike accident that turned deadly when the symptoms of that concussion refused to go away. The condition is known as post-concussion syndrome (PCS), suffered frequently by boxers, hockey and football players, and middle-aged adventurists like me who have hit their head one too many times.

If you've ever had a concussion, you know these are not symptoms you want hanging around: sensitivity to light and sound, mood swings, and a constant ringing inside your head. It's the kind of torture I could not have imagined enduring for a day, let alone a month. But I did, for five months. To give you some idea of what this pain is like, imagine the static sound emitted during one of those emergency broadcast tests on your television set. Now imagine that sound turned up as loud as your TV will go. You reach for the volume to crank it down, but it doesn't work. You try to leave your apartment but the doors are locked. There's no escaping the auditory onslaught, so you simply sit down to endure this 60 seconds from hell. But it doesn't go away after 60 seconds. It keeps blaring, for an entire hour, then a week, then a month, then several months. That was my experience with PCS—the only relief coming with complete isolation, hanging blackout curtains on windows, and sleeping on a floor in a bedroom closet. After five impossibly long months, a simple realization came: if this is as good as my health gets, I will not live long; *I am staring at the last chapter of my life.*

It's a powerful thing to face your own death, how mortality can move one into action. And once I surrendered, a single thought came to mind: *you cannot die without ever having told your story; you cannot die without ever having expressed who you truly are.* You see, I had been changing my life for some 15 years, having woken up from our collective sleep, awakened to a vision of the world and how it works, to my own hypocrisy and the hypocrisy of a culture operating in opposition to that vision—a culture that has become lost in, as Thomas Merton said, *"the murderous din of our materialism."* I was raised in this culture of excess, seduced by its empty charms and deluded into unconscious behaviors that I am now hopefully, prayerfully, and imperfectly undoing in an attempt to leave consumerism for compassion and move from material wealth to true wealth. By the grace of life, or dare I say God,* a new perspective has come. So I offer this writing as part confession and part communiqué of the ideas that now inhabit me, to all who might feel that life can be simpler, deeper, and richer than the current cultural vision we now robotically move to in lockstep march.

So what became of our hiker friends? We did see them again, a chance meeting at a local convenience store, where they told us the gas was so needed in those subfreezing temperatures that the initial shock at the sight of the unlikely messenger was soon overshadowed by the utility of the goods delivered. Perhaps it will be the same here—that the shock at this unlikely messenger will soon be dwarfed by whatever fuel this book offers, by the light it may provide and the principles illuminated herein. For it is in principles and principles alone that you and I will right humanity's wayward course and begin to birth the loving, kind, and compassionate world we all dream is possible. Our view of the world and its troubles has become unnecessarily complex and convoluted, and we're now collectively overwhelmed and discouraged about what each of us can do to turn the tide on the world's woes. War, poverty, genocide, and the environmental crisis cast far too black and wide a shadow to ever be solved by any single person, simple idea, or concept. But consider this:

---

* Author's note: In this text, I have chosen to use the word *God* as it is simply the best word I know to talk about the Mystery, Source, Creator, The Force, Life, Love, or The Big Electron, as George Carlin used to call it. The "G" word is not meant to favor any particular religion, or to conjure up stereotypical images of a man with a white beard sitting in judgment on a throne. It is an attempt to articulate the impossible; the indefinable, uncontainable divine spark; the fire that burns without consuming, in you and me and in all living things. Please substitute in your head and heart whatever word/expression is comfortable for you.

war, poverty, genocide, and the environmental crisis are not really the problem at all; they are *symptoms* of a deeper endemic problem, which, if identified and held up to the light, *can be solved.* It's been said that the definition of intelligence is the ability to identify primary causes. That's my intention here, to identify the primary cause of the world's ills and in so doing, to state plainly the solution and empower each of us to be a part of this desperately needed corrective course.

✳

A WORD OF WARNING: If you're reading *Life's Operating Manual* hoping to discover the ten steps to fix your life, you're in for a disappointment. This book is not about ten steps; it's about one: understanding the simple but significant principle that, when truly embraced and embodied, changes everything. Ralph Waldo Emerson understood this all too well. He left the Unitarian ministry to write about it; he communicated it to Harvard's Divinity School and was not invited back for 30 years. Virtually all of his essays and lectures, when boiled down to their essence, are about this one idea. The same can be said of Gandhi's writings; Martin Luther King, Jr.'s speeches; the teachings of Lao Tzu; and the poetry of Rumi. It is an idea that crosses space and time, cultural upbringings and religious divides; it is an idea that can shoot an arrow of infinite understanding into your heart. Remember, the Buddha was not said to be wise, but awake. That is the hope of this book: to awaken the reader, to lay bare this idea, this principle, in all of its simplicity, power, and perfection.

A few years ago, I helped found a homeless shelter in Charlottesville, Virginia. When our efforts were met with some resistance, I said to Charlie Woods, a homeless man, urging his patience: "Charlie, we're trying our best to get the community to understand the homeless." Charlie countered, "People have been *under* standing the homeless for far too long. What we need is for people to *over* stand." When it comes to what's gone wrong in the world and how we can fix it, I side with Mr. Woods; we have been *under* standing for far too long. This book is my attempt to *over* stand.

INTRODUCTION:
TWO WOLVES INSIDE US

*

*If you would be a real seeker after truth,
it is necessary that at least once in your life,
you doubt, as far as possible, all things.*

—RENÉ DESCARTES

TODAY'S ACTION MOVIES, from *Star Wars* to *Transformers*, owe a great deal to our ancient ancestors who passed down stories of the ongoing battle between light and darkness, good and evil, angels and demons. One of my favorites is a popular Native American myth about two wolves that live inside each of us, two wolves engaged in a fierce battle for control of our lives. One wolf, *the fearful wolf,* walks in anger, ego, envy, greed, resentment, and lies. The other wolf, *the truthful wolf,* lives in appreciation, kindness, love, joy, compassion, and empathy. For far too long, I have listened to my fearful wolf hollering its bad advice: *"You have to fit in! Don't rock the boat! Do as you're told!"* But thankfully, over time, the wolf of my truth has stood up to his illusory twin, silencing this dark shouter with simple whispers of wisdom: *"Seek the truth. Follow your heart. Let go."* Is it any surprise then, that much of this book came to me as a conversation between these two internal, warring voices, voices I call simply *Fear* and *Truth?*

The Sufi mystics, the ascetics of the Muslim faith, believe there are three ways of approaching the divine: one way is prayer, a step up from that is meditation, and a step up from that is conversation. The unique structure of *Life's Operating Manual* was conceived with this Sufi admonition in mind. Here's how the book lays out: each chapter begins with a short essay that offers my thoughts on the various challenges we face as individuals and a society in order to birth a more kind and compassionate world. Each essay is then followed by a conversation—*the Fear and Truth dialogues*—that tests my suppositions and their application in the real world. The format is not unlike a classroom with a lesson plan and an ensuing question-and-answer period. The only difference being—and it's quite a difference!—both participating voices are my own; my own fear challenging my own truth.

Understand, *the Fear and Truth dialogues* are not an exercise in good angel/bad angel; Fear is not bad, nor Truth, good. Fear simply is, and as you will see, it has its place and purpose. Furthermore, the voices of Fear and Truth are not meant to represent everyone's fear, and all truth. Fear is the voice of fear as it exists/existed in me. The hope here is it will prove relatable and recognizable. Truth is simply how God, Source, Life, is presently working through me. And while I do not speak for all fear, and make no claim to know the whole truth and nothing but the truth, these are two characters I have come to know well: Fear, in my days of holding on, and Truth, as I've learned to let go. Directing films, I have discovered, is very much about letting go. *But,* you say, *directors are control freaks!* Certainly. But when we are at our best, we are simply good listeners, we get out of the way of the work and creativity unfolds. Fear represents our need to hang on to the riverbank, to control outcomes, results, our lives; it swims upstream. Truth is about releasing that hold, letting go of results, and trusting the direction of Life's current. I hope the ensuing dialogues will prove instructive and help the reader loosen his grip on the shoreline, and fall headlong into the river's flow.

Now, back to our Native American myth about the warring wolves: *"Which wolf wins?"* you ask, *"the wolf of Fear, or the wolf of Truth?"* The answer is simple: *"The one you feed . . ."* May these dialogues feed your own authenticity, further encourage your walk into truth, into your own heart, and thereby, into the Heart of All.

❋

THE FOLLOWING IS a sample dialogue provoked by the book's preface where I state plainly my intention to offer a perspective on a world gone wrong. Take a look:

FEAR: So you're writing a book? Ha! You and everyone else.
TRUTH: I am not concerned with everyone else. That's your territory.

FEAR: But you have no qualifications. You're just a comedy director.
TRUTH: A comedy director is not who I am.

FEAR: Okay, fine. You write and teach, as well.
TRUTH: These are things I do. They are not who I am.

FEAR: Then who are you?
TRUTH: This is the subject of the book, the question we must all answer: *who are you?*

FEAR: And you have something new to say on the topic?
TRUTH: The essence is not new. It's been said before. For billions of years.

FEAR: Billions of years? Man just learned to speak 100,000 years ago! See, you are already showing your ignorance.
TRUTH: Is speech limited to man? Do the stars not speak? Does the sun not praise?

FEAR: They don't speak like we speak.
TRUTH: Perhaps, better. That's what Thomas Merton believed.

FEAR: The monk? He lived in silence. What does he know about speech?
TRUTH: He heard God talk in the trees.

FEAR: Then he was out of his mind.
TRUTH: Precisely. And in his heart.

FEAR: You're missing the point. What right does the director of *Ace Ventura* have to tell people how to live?
TRUTH: No right. I wish to tell no one how to live. I simply share what I know.

FEAR: But your hope is to change people, admit it!
TRUTH: My hope is to provide a perspective. The results are not up to me.

FEAR: Good, because people won't change. Even your religions say people are flawed, that people are fallen.
TRUTH: People are not fallen. They have forgotten.

FEAR: Forgotten? Forgotten what?
TRUTH: Who they are.

FEAR: That again! Are there no other questions to ask? Fine, write your book. I won't remain silent, you know. I will speak my mind.
TRUTH: You will speak *from* the mind, certainly.

FEAR: And what's wrong with that? Our minds are what make us different. Descartes said, I think therefore I am.
TRUTH: And I say, *I AM therefore I think.*

FEAR: You confuse me. What is it you want to accomplish here?
TRUTH: Nothing. It is already accomplished.

FEAR: Now you sound like a Christian touting the saving grace of Jesus.
TRUTH: This is not about Christianity, or any other faith, for that matter. It's about answering the question—

FEAR: I know, I know! Who are you?
TRUTH: Yes. *Who are you?* Shall we find out?

THE WORLD IS BROKEN

✳

*A new type of thinking is essential
if mankind is to survive . . .*

—ALBERT EINSTEIN

I HAVE LONG SAID that all of my best friends are dead. And by best friends, I mean those with whom I have spent a great deal of time, who have poured light into my soul, who have recognized my true identity—whose words, thoughts, and deeds have inspired me to new heights of love and understanding. I'm speaking of those radical, ragamuffin spirits, Jesus, Gandhi, Lao Tzu, Emerson, Thoreau, Hafiz, Rumi, Kahlil Gibran, Thomas Merton, St. Francis of Assisi, Rainer Maria Rilke, and Martin Luther King, Jr. But there is one exception to this funereal list of saints and sages, writers and philosophers; she is a Pulitzer Prize–winning poet, and she is very much alive. Her name is Mary Oliver, and in 2007 I had the blessed opportunity to speak with her. Here's how it happened.

Show business, and the arts in general, are not unlike a supper club. We often reach out to one another to share not only a meal, but a conversation, about craft, mentoring, and the possibility of working together. For years, I reached out to Mary with the singular hope of basking in her light. Her poetry had long buoyed my soul, the beauty she sensed even in the mundane (especially the mundane!)—electric light perceived in a blade of grass or virtue in a stone. Two years had passed since my initial attempt at contact, to no avail—I had asked "my people" to call "her people," a big mistake when dealing with a sage! Then, one day, a friend shared some disturbing news: Mary Oliver was in financial trouble and was in danger of losing her house. I was aware that Mary's life partner of 47 years had just passed from a difficult bout with cancer and thought perhaps this was the source of her distress. Whatever the reason, it was unacceptable—Mary Oliver was my heart; her words, her art, her spirit had done so much for so many, I had to do all I could to help. I immediately called her booking agent and let him know of my intention. This was the first he had heard of Mary's difficulties and agreed to assess the situation. Five minutes later, the phone rang; it was Mary herself. She told me she was, in fact, financially fine, and then expressed her appreciation for the kindness extended. We talked briefly about her work; I shared the depth of inspiration and influence her poetry had brought to my life; and then, unprompted, as we were wrapping up the call, she said, "*The world is broken, Tom. You know that, don't you?*" This stopped me. Ten simple words, spoken directly, with such sureness, they cut me to the core. Not because she expressed something new, but rather, something I already knew, a truth that had long been burning inside me. "*The world is broken, Tom. You know that, don't you?*" I did know. Many of us know it, too. The world we see around us remains engulfed in war, genocide, hunger, inequity, and environmental devastation. These ruinous, recurring trends are telling. Something is deeply wrong.

What is it? What exactly has gone wrong? Is mankind just a flawed species doomed to destroy itself and the natural world?

Are these violent, aggressive, and selfish tendencies just who we are, or is there something we're missing, some idea or perspective that can shift our world from broken to beatific?

Dialogue One:

FEAR: Mary Oliver. Another dreamer. Her poetry even questions ambition.

TRUTH: Yes, a wonderful idea. As she writes:

"What will ambition do for me that the fox, appearing suddenly
at the top of the field,
her eyes sharp and confident as she stared into mine,
has not already done?"

FEAR: She wishes to be like the fox in the field? She wishes for nothing greater?

TRUTH: And what is greater than the fox in the field, open and attentive to the present hour? Content with who and what she is?

FEAR: Contentment is overrated. If you are content, you have no ambition. Our schools teach children to be ambitious so they'll act, they'll do things in the world.

TRUTH: And what is it you wish children to be ambitious for?

FEAR: For anything. For everything.

TRUTH: So ambition is good in and of itself? Like your belief in technology?

FEAR: What is wrong with technology? You cannot deny that it is good!

TRUTH: Technology is not good. And it is not bad. It is neutral. The same cell phone that connects a person in love can be used to set off a car bomb. The same technology that allows the free exchange of ideas can be used to harass and bully.

FEAR: Technology saves lives! It connects people from across the globe! It moves civilization forward!

TRUTH: Ah yes, civilization. That thing the human race will eventually die of.

FEAR: This is a tired sentiment. From Emerson. Emerson was wrong. Civilization has saved man.

TRUTH: If man's current mind-set does not change, the mind-set that undergirds today's civilization, man, along with civilization, will indeed die off.

FEAR: And what is this mind-set?

TRUTH: It has a lot to do with ambition.

FEAR: What?! Everything that has ever been invented, created, forged has come from someone's ambition. Do you not see this?

TRUTH: Was Jesus ambitious?

FEAR: I'm sure he was.

TRUTH: And what was he ambitious for?

FEAR: I don't know. Recruiting disciples. Or even cheesier, spreading love.

TRUTH: What about Gandhi?

FEAR: His ambition was political, to unite India.

TRUTH: To unite all men.

FEAR: So what? Why this quiz?

TRUTH: Because the question is not, *"Are* you ambitious?" The question is, *"What* are you ambitious for?" If you are ambitious for personal gain, money, power, fame, glory, and material possessions, can you say then that ambition is good?

FEAR: Your example is negative. What about a positive ambition? Say, if a young man wants to be president.

TRUTH: And why is this ambition positive, why is it good?

FEAR: He wants to be president, as in President of the United States!

TRUTH: You have not answered the question. You have told me he wants to be president, not *why* he wants to be president.

FEAR: What does it matter why? It is the most powerful position in the world!

TRUTH: It is not the most powerful position in the world. The woman who raises her child in love and gratitude is as powerful, if not more so.

FEAR: Ridiculous. The President of the United States affects millions.
TRUTH: As does the child raised in love.

FEAR: The child cannot send us to war.
TRUTH: He can acquiesce to that war or resist it. Both actions have power.

FEAR: Still nothing close to the power of the president!
TRUTH: You are blind, Fear, because you, like many today, only see in terms of size. You believe something has to be big to be powerful or effective. It is the idolatry of magnitude, and it is a poison, a lie.

FEAR: What does any of this have to do with a child who wants to be president?
TRUTH: You see ambition as positive, especially if a child has ambition to reach the heights of the presidency. But if he is ambitious for power, the presidency is not a height, but a pit. And he is part of the present-day mind-set that will lead to our ruin.

FEAR: You do not know such a mind-set will lead to anyone's ruin.
TRUTH: It has always led to ruin. History is full of extinct civilizations, civilizations that have chosen ambition over awareness. It is not how nature works; it is not what makes nature thrive.

FEAR: Nature. So we are back to Mary Oliver.
TRUTH: And the fox in the field.

FEAR: The fox with no ambition.
TRUTH: The fox with the only true ambition.

FEAR: Which is what?
TRUTH: To be what she already is.

THE CRISIS OF OUR TIME

✳

*What can we gain by sailing to the moon if we are not able
to cross the abyss that separates us from ourselves?*

—THOMAS MERTON

THE GRAPH BELOW is an approximation, representing the
175,000-year history of the human species. The solid black line
indicates the basic, common trajectory of population growth,
technological advances, and environmental destruction (such as
deforestation, species loss, carbon emissions, and the prevalence
of toxic pollution in our air, oceans, and water supply).

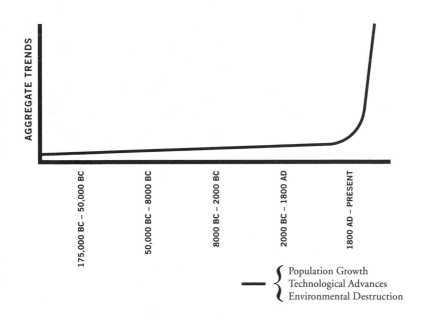

Notice the gradual ascent, the black line slowly trending upward from the dawn of man until 1800. Population increases are remarkably gradual, taking 174,800 years to reach our first billion.* In fact, just two thousand years ago, at the time of Christ, there were only 250 million people on the planet. But look at what happens after 1800. It takes just 123 years to reach our second billion, just 33 to reach our third, and 15 to reach our fourth. We have now crossed the seven-billion mark, and by 2027 we are expected to top eight billion. The same gradual ascent is evident with our developing technologies. Innovation moves along slowly and steadily for most of mankind's history with the discovery of fire, the invention of the wheel, the forging of metal, the rise of agriculture, and eventually the invention of the printing press. But look at what happens, again around 1800, just after the dawn of the Industrial Revolution. From here, technological progress begins a sharp ascent, with the discovery of electricity, and the invention of the steam engine, the telegraph, the telephone, the automobile, airplane travel, space travel, the computer, cell phones, and the Internet. And in direct correlation with this technological revolution and the population explosion came the widespread pollution of the natural world, the accelerated loss of species and habitat, and the possibility that mankind, through carbon emissions, is heating up the planet with catastrophic consequences.

---

* Author's note: It's hard to pinpoint exactly how far back the human species dates. Some trace our origins back one to two million years, but conservative estimates land in the range of 175,000 years. For the purposes of this book, we'll err on the conservative side, and agree that humankind is 175,000 years old.

The second graph is also an approximation, if such a graph could exist, with the gray line representing the moral and ethical advances of the human species over that same 175,000 years.

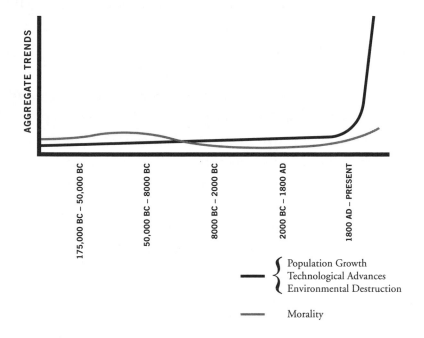

Of course, morality is not so easily measured—here, it refers to mankind's overall movement as a species toward love, compassion, peace, and harmony—and this attempt certainly has its limits. However, a reasonable assessment of the trending of human ethics does reveal an alarming deficiency. Around 2000 BC, we begin to observe an overall, slow moral progression: laws become codified; slavery is eventually, legally abolished; racism in most nations becomes taboo, as does discrimination based on sexual orientation; women fight for equal rights with men and gain positions of power in many governments.* But again, notice what happens around 1800. While environmental destruction, population growth, and technological advances have skyrocketed, our morals and ethics have not responded in kind. Martin Luther King, Jr. saw this growing chasm and recognized its potential peril in his 1964 Nobel Prize acceptance speech:

In spite of these spectacular strides in science and technology, and still unlimited ones to come, something basic is missing. There is a sort of poverty of the spirit which stands in glaring contrast to our scientific and technological abundance. The richer we have become materially, the poorer we have become morally and spiritually. We have learned to fly the air like birds and swim the sea like fish, but we have not learned the simple art of living together as brothers . . . Enlarged material powers spell enlarged peril if there is not proportionate growth of the soul.

It is my contention that the failure of morality and ethics to keep pace with mankind's technological and population explosions is the most significant crisis of our time. Mary Oliver's reminder that the world is broken, and Martin Luther King, Jr.'s warning of the danger inherent in our ethical inertia, are admonitions that demand our consideration. The question

---

* Author's note: The gradually ascending gray line beginning on the left axis of the second graph also notes moral advances among early indigenous people, the many tribes that embraced unity and oneness with the natural world—ideologies that were obliterated or shifted after the arrival of agriculture around 8,000 BC (to be discussed in detail in a later chapter).

we must ask now is, *Can we change? What will it take to birth a moral revolution as dramatic and impactful as our technological revolution? What is it that has our morality lagging so dramatically behind our technology?*

Dialogue Two:

FEAR: So you are preaching revolution? Your aim is not only high, but unrealistically so.
TRUTH: You do not believe revolution is possible?

FEAR: Not only is it not possible, you are 200 years too late. America has already had her revolution.
TRUTH: The American Revolution was not a revolution. Not in the truest sense.

FEAR: The American Revolution was not a revolution? Tell that to the soldiers with muskets, to the crowds cheering in the streets!
TRUTH: A true revolution does not begin with guns, or cheering in the streets. It begins on the inside, in silence.

FEAR: Well congratulations, you have just lost your readers! And it only took you 25 pages!
TRUTH: The revolution you speak of was, indeed, a turn in the road. But we were still on the same road. In business, men still took advantage of one another, still enslaved one another; in worldly affairs, men still desired conquest. True, America was no

longer ruled by the king, but she was still ruled by that which ruled the king.

FEAR: And what ruled the king?
TRUTH: What rules to this day, a mind-set that is ruinous. A true revolution is more radical. The word *radical* means "root," and we have not gotten to the root of things.

FEAR: So tell me, what is the "root" of things? What do you consider a true revolution?
TRUTH: When the earth makes one revolution in a 24-hour period, it has turned completely around. This is what is needed. We must turn things completely around.

FEAR: And how will you do this, how will you turn things completely around? Like this moral gap, what you call the crisis of our time.
TRUTH: The crisis of our time is not the moral gap, but the mentality that has allowed the moral gap to arise in the first place.

FEAR: And this mentality, this is the crisis that causes all others crises?
TRUTH: Yes.

FEAR: So this causes war?
TRUTH: Yes.

FEAR: And genocide?
TRUTH: Yes.

FEAR: And hunger?

TRUTH: And poverty, and greed, and the economic crisis, and the housing collapse, and skyrocketing suicide rates, and the environmental crisis. Shall I go on?

FEAR: But if your graph is true, that man has not evolved morally, what hope does he have to fix what you call this broken world? Isn't this just an indication of who he is, flawed and defective? His selfish behavior consistently written on the pages of history?

TRUTH: If these same crises showed up in all other cultures, perhaps yes; perhaps then the pages of history would convict man. But they do not. Until the West arrived, there had never been a poor person in Ladakh, not as we define poverty. Genocide is virtually unheard of in tribal and indigenous communities. The San Bushmen of the Kalahari Desert have never developed weapons of war. If people are who they are, by nature flawed and defective, why do these problems not show up in these other cultures?

FEAR: Is this why you have this idealistic notion about people, that they are capable of change?

TRUTH: You don't believe people are capable of change? Are there not times in history when enough evidence surfaces that the majority of people shift their thinking and behavior?

FEAR: Perhaps, but these are rare.

TRUTH: In fact, examples are plentiful. Doctors once thought frontal lobotomies were helpful in controlling psychosis. Are you familiar with this?

FEAR: Of course, in the 1930s and '40s. For two decades, lobotomies were a mainstream procedure, prescribed with regularity.

TRUTH: But today, they are rarely performed. What changed that?

FEAR: They found out they did more harm than good. They found out they didn't work.

TRUTH: Right, they didn't work. So people changed their behavior. And what about the history of cigarettes? When cigarettes were first introduced, smoking was believed to be relaxing and healthy. Even doctors recommended cigarettes to their patients. Since then, millions have quit smoking. Why? What made countless people suffer through the pain of breaking this most powerful addiction?

FEAR: They discovered that smoking causes cancer. They discovered that cigarettes can kill you.

TRUTH: Right. People understood this. There was little debate and so they stopped. Their behavior changed . . . Why can't the same happen with their view of the world? If people are shown that their behavior is harmful, even worse than smoking, wouldn't they want to stop?

FEAR: You will have a hard time proving this.

TRUTH: But if it *can* be demonstrated, wouldn't many people want to change?

FEAR: I suppose. But you will need volumes to convince them. And they will never read volumes.
TRUTH: Volumes are not needed. You only need to consider how life works.

FEAR: So, enlighten me. How does it work?
TRUTH: This is the subject of our exploration.

FEAR: Can you not offer a clue now? How does life work?
TRUTH: Here is your clue: it works perfectly.

FEAR: Perfectly?! The world is a mess! The world is unjust!
TRUTH: The world is perfectly just. When people care about the things they care about, when they set themselves against each other in competition and strife, the world becomes a perfect reflection of that behavior. The world is just as people have created it to be.

FEAR: If the world is perfectly just, then why do you want to change it?
TRUTH: Changing the world is not what I want. The world is perfectly fine. And it will go on perfectly well without us.

FEAR: So it is people you want to change?
TRUTH: No, people do not need to change.

FEAR: How can you say that? Look at your morality graph! People are greedy, selfish, and violent! You cannot be happy with who they are.
TRUTH: Who they are is not the problem. It is that they have lost

touch with who they are. Violence, greed, selfishness—these grow out of human forgetfulness, out of a belief in masks and illusions. Once people awaken to what is—to who they are, to reality—these behaviors will fall away.

FEAR: But you still want people to wake up, which means you want them to change.

TRUTH: And herein lies the paradox: the world will change, people will change, when they realize who they are can never change.

LIFE'S OPERATING MANUAL

✴

The world is not to be put in order; the world is in order.
It is for us to put ourselves in unison with this order.

—HENRY MILLER

IN THE SUMMER OF 2011, I was asked to give a presentation to 800 teenagers at a conference sponsored by Invisible Children, a youth-oriented charity focused on freeing child soldiers and ending Africa's longest-running war. The talk was called *Life's Operating Manual,* and consisted of a slide show that began with an image of a man pouring coffee on his computer keyboard. Yes, that's right, a man purposely dousing his laptop in hot java. Not a good idea, as indicated by the laughter and audible cringing from the audience. *"What would happen if a person tried to turn on their computer this way?"* I asked the still-settling crowd. Various shouts rang out: *"You'd ruin it!" "You'd fry the thing!" "Kiss your keyboard goodbye!" "Why?"* I shot back. *"Why would you ruin it?"* Someone quickly shouted, *"Because that's not how you turn on a computer! That's not how a computer works!"* All nodded in agreement. *"Right!"* I said. *"And how do people know how a computer works?" "People just know!"* another teen called out. *"Not at first, they don't,"* I countered. *"People have to get this information from somewhere. Where do they get it?"* There was a long thoughtful pause, then a young man called out, framing his answer in the form of a question: *"From the computer's operating manual?" "Right!"* I exclaimed.

"A computer comes with an operating manual! And this manual tells you how the computer works!" All nodded in agreement. *"It tells you to keep it in a cool dry place; it tells you to plug it into the right power source; it tells you to keep it relatively dust free. And why does it tell you these things?"* The audience had caught on by now: *"Because that's what's good for a computer! It's how your computer works."* *"Not just works,"* I said, *"but works what . . . ?"* *"Well!"* a student shouted. *"Works well!"* *"Exactly! It's how your computer works well. You might even say, it's how your computer thrives. It's all in this thing we call the operating manual."*

I then clicked the small remote in my hand, and the next slide appeared—an iconic image of the earth, the big blue-green ball floating serenely in space. I pointed to the magical planet we call home, and posed this question: *"Is it possible that this, too, comes with an operating manual?"* Dead silence. Most had never thought about it this way. *"And if we knew what was written inside that manual, would we not know what makes this* (I pointed to the planet) *work well?"* Slowly, heads started to nod, warming to the idea. I challenged them further: *"If such an operating manual does exist, where would you look for it?"* Puzzled expressions dotted the room. *"It's not complicated."* I said. *"If you want to know how a computer works, you look at a computer, right? And if you want to know how life works, you look at what?"* Suddenly, they understood: *"Life!"* they shouted as one. *"And what exactly do you mean by life? What exactly would you look at?"* I asked. Answers came quickly: *"Nature!"* *"The ocean!"* *"A rain forest!"* *"Biology!"* *"Us!"* *"Yes,"* I said, *"you would look at us, nature, all of it, from single cells to multicelled creatures; from biology to the biosphere. You'd look at an oak tree and an ant colony. You'd look at a human being and a hummingbird. And what exactly would you be looking for?"* Another thoughtful pause, then: *"You'd look for what makes life work well."* *"Yes,"* I said with some satisfaction. *"You'd look for the common principles that support life, the principles and behaviors that make life thrive."*

Does an operating manual for life exist? I believe that it does—a belief I share with Emerson, Gandhi, Martin Luther King, Jr., and others. Its commands are not written on paper, but rather in the stars, in planetary rotations, in fields of grass, in you and in me. Evidence is not in short supply; nature has had four billion years to communicate her principles, daily demonstrating the mechanics of life, the laws of existence, which are both moral and physical. When I interviewed Desmond Tutu for *I AM*, I asked him the question I posed to all of the interviewees: *"What's wrong with the world?"* Archbishop Tutu said this: *"Tom, God gave us instructions on the box of this thing we call 'human being.' We are not following the instructions on the box."* By "instructions on the box," he was not referring to the Bible, or any religious dogma. He was talking about principles, ethics, and values; he was talking about how things work; he was talking about life's operating manual. The question before us now is, can we discern those "instructions on the box"? Can we, with reasonable certainty, determine what exactly makes human life, all of life, thrive? Can we "read" life's operating manual, and as important, garner the courage and clarity to live in accordance with its precepts?

Dialogue Three:

FEAR: *Life's Operating Manual* is clever, but it is unrealistic.
TRUTH: It is unrealistic to offer a point of view on how things work?

FEAR: It is unrealistic to say the solutions to the world's problems can be contained in any one manual. They are far too complicated.
TRUTH: Actually an entire manual is not needed. A paragraph would do.

FEAR: War, famine, genocide? You claim to have the answer to all of these? You can end hunger?
TRUTH: People can end hunger, yes.

FEAR: So, why haven't they?
TRUTH: They think hunger is a matter of money, of creating the right program, or planting the right seeds. They look at it mechanistically. But hunger will not be solved through mechanics, but a mind-set. The mind of man must change; then hunger will change.

FEAR: This is another problem with your manual. Like all religious manuals, you wish to control minds, to control people.
TRUTH: I do not wish to control people. I wish only to inform them.

FEAR: Inform them of what?
TRUTH: Their power.

FEAR: What power? People have no real power. Not over these global problems.

TRUTH: This is a great deception. That people are powerless.

FEAR: What power does an individual have against a global corporation?

TRUTH: He has the power to withdraw his power.

FEAR: And what good will that do? Even governments are controlled by corporations.

TRUTH: So corporations are all powerful?

FEAR: Everyone knows this.

TRUTH: And where does this power come from?

FEAR: Where all power comes from, money! They make billions.

TRUTH: And where does this money come from?

(A long pause…)

FEAR: It comes from people.

TRUTH: Yes, it comes from people. No corporation has any power that people don't give it. No government has any power that people don't grant it. When people understand that corporations are a reflection of their own energy, and when they assume responsibility for that energy, corporate omnipotence will be seen for what it is, an illusion.

FEAR: So now you are doing away with corporate power? What's next, war?
TRUTH: A wonderful idea.

FEAR: Ha! Just like one of your movies, you speak of impossible happy endings. I prefer real-life endings, and real-life endings are not happy.
TRUTH: More deception.

FEAR: What deception? Real life is full of darkness! Death, divorce, separation, loss, pain, suffering. The things that await us all at the end of our story.
TRUTH: These things are not at the end of any story.

FEAR: Of course they are, death is the end of life, divorce is the end of marriage. What—you would have happiness come out of death, out of loss? That's what Hollywood does; that's not what life does.
TRUTH: It is exactly what life does. It goes on. The story continues. The story tends upward, toward unity, toward love.

FEAR: How does the story tend toward love for a boy killed in the gas chambers of Auschwitz?
TRUTH: You have ended his story too soon. Read on: unity and resolve soon overcome Hitler, cries of *never again* ring out worldwide, love to this day rises up in response to racism and hatred—the boy's story continues, the boy's story tends toward love.

FEAR: This is Hollywood talking again. Tying everything in a neat bow.

TRUTH: It is *life* talking, and the bow is not neat. It is messy, and beautiful, and blessed.

FEAR: What is blessed about a boy's death or any death for that matter?

TRUTH: You see death as an ending. I see it as a beginning. Just as the poet says, *"What have I ever lost by dying?"*

FEAR: And like all poets, this Rumi is insane!

TRUTH: Or is it insane when you have become attached to the flesh, to that which comes from dust and will return to dust? For the mystic, death is a doorway—the doorway to amazement.

FEAR: It is the doorway to pain.

TRUTH: Yes, and the pain it brings fuels passion for life, for love, and for the expansion of beauty in the world. Until you can see the beauty of death, the *illusion* of death, you will not know who you really are.

FEAR: Does knowing who you are take away the pain of a mother who has lost her only son?

TRUTH: I do not wish to take away the pain. Only to give it perspective.

FEAR: I do not understand. You talk about life and how it works. But for many it does not work.

TRUTH: Fear, you see only in the short term. Your vision is myopic. If you could look beyond, you would see that life does indeed work, and quite well. The boy's story is a sound example. Hate may rise up for a time, but love will always overcome it.

FEAR: But why this talk about how life works? I thought this book is about answering the question, who are you?

TRUTH: If you know how life works, you will know who you are. And if you know who you are, you will know how life works.

FEAR: Who you are and how life works are one and the same?

TRUTH: Now you are catching on.

TWO MASTERS

✳

*Their whole generation adopted false principles,
and went to their graves in the belief they were
enriching the country which they were impoverishing.*

—RALPH WALDO EMERSON

I LOVE LANGUAGE. And I love how truth can reveal itself in words, which, upon close examination, can awaken us to new meaning and purpose. The word *mortgage,* for example, means *death pledge* (from the Latin, *mort,* meaning *death,* and *gage, to pledge*). So when you take out a mortgage, you're signing a death pledge! *Courage* is from two French words, *coeur,* which means *heart,* and *âge.* So, *courage* means, *age of the heart!* And the word *community* is a beautiful combination of two words, *come + unity.*

So, it shouldn't have surprised me when I looked up the word *hypocrite* and found it originated from the Greek word *hypokrites,* meaning, *actor.* As a movie director and former acting teacher, I know exactly what it means to be an actor: an actor is *someone who lives truthfully under imaginary circumstances.* In fact, it's my job as a director to give an actor those imaginary circumstances, and it's the actor's job to behave as if those circumstances are true. I bring this up because, for much of my adult life, I've been a hypocrite. Please understand, this is not something I was aware of, but something I woke up to recently, after much examination and introspection. On the stage of life you might say, I was an actor: someone or something was giving me imaginary circumstances, and I was behaving as if those circumstances were true.

Let me fall on the sword here and fill in some of my hypocritical specifics. First and foremost, I have always considered myself a spiritual person. Since I was a boy, I have found the teachings of Jesus on love and compassion powerful and true. I had little interest in the dogma of religion, which, as Thomas Aquinas said, "seems like straw," and felt as Thomas Merton did, that I need not dogma but the living God. Rather, it was the unifying ideals of the major faiths that spoke to me: *"Do unto others as you would have them do unto you," "Love your neighbor as yourself,"* and even *"Love your enemy";* and I decided at an early age to dedicate my life to those same principles.

For years, I prayed and journaled every morning, and soaked myself in the words of Jesus, Lao Tzu, Thomas Merton, Ralph Waldo Emerson, Henry David Thoreau, Mahatma Gandhi, Rainer Maria Rilke, the Desert Fathers, Henri Nouwen, Madeleine L'Engle, Mary Oliver, Walt Whitman, Rumi, and Hafiz. I attended church most Sundays and checked myself into Merton's monastery in Kentucky to live in silence and experience the life of a Trappist monk. And when I formed Shady Acres, at Universal (My company was named after the insane asylum in *Ace Ventura*—little did I know how appropriate that title would turn out to be!), I set up a charity division to oversee the disbursement of money to worthy causes.

And yet, even with my sights set on Jesus and Gandhi, somehow I lived—what do they say these days?—large. My films, after all, had grossed roughly two billion dollars, and to the victor belonged the spoils. (There's another word, *spoils*, the root of which is *spoil!*) I flew privately everywhere and anywhere I pleased. I bought expensive houses, antiques, and old masters' paintings at Sotheby's auctions, and paid tens of thousands of dollars for authentic Persian rugs. Remarkably, I saw no conflict between this lifestyle and my beliefs in the ethics of the saints and sages. Nor did anyone else in my world. Rather, I was held up as a model of success, of someone who had made it, and even made it with a sense of goodness and conscience. I had learned well from my culture and took all I could—far exceeding my needs and in contradiction to my spiritual mentors and teachers across the ages. How? How had I, a lover of Jesus, who was told not to store up treasures on earth where moth and rust destroy, become a poster boy for material success, where I stored up lots of treasure on earth, giving moth and rust plenty to destroy? How had I, who knew you cannot serve two masters, God and money, done his darnedest to do just that? How had I, who decried the gap between the rich and the poor, *become* the gap between the rich and the poor? And as important, how did all these things happen without my conscious awareness or the awareness of those around me?

Dialogue Four:

FEAR: I don't understand you. What is your complaint? You won at the game! You were rich!

TRUTH: And in some ways, quite poor. As the poet has said, *"I don't think there is such a thing as an intelligent mega-rich person. For* *who with a fine mind can look out upon this world and hoard what can nourish a thousand souls?"*

FEAR: The Sufi, Kabir! He is a dreamer like the rest. Who is he to judge the wealthy? Who is he to say this money made you a bad person?

TRUTH: I was not a bad person. I was simply asleep. Asleep to the needs of others; asleep to my effect on the natural world; asleep to who I am and how things work.

FEAR: How things work? I'd say they worked beautifully. You were well off.

TRUTH: I had money and things. There is a difference.

FEAR: I don't understand you. What is wrong with making as much money as you can? You can give it all away if you want.

TRUTH: You would have me take all I can regardless of what effect this has on others? You would have me demand millions, while the maintenance man and the cleaning crew cannot feed their families?

FEAR: Yes. Take it all, and give what you wish to the maintenance man and the cleaning crew!

TRUTH: This logic is a poison. Why be greedy now to be generous later?

FEAR: Because the end justifies the means, that's why.

TRUTH: The end does not justify the means. The means are the end.

FEAR: So you would let the corporation keep all of this money? Don't you see how naïve this is?

TRUTH: Then Jesus was naïve, as was Gandhi. Both could have undoubtedly charged for their speeches and with the profit, fed the hungry and clothed the naked. But they gave of themselves freely. Why? Because they knew that money would never solve hunger; love would.

FEAR: And money is one way we can love!

TRUTH: But it is not loving to ask for all of it, to ask for more than you need.

FEAR: But people work hard. You work hard. You got what you deserved.

TRUTH: Including stress, diminished health, and disconnection from my true self and those around me.

FEAR: You act like you had some kind of a disease.

TRUTH: The Native Americans called it *wetiko*. It means, one who eats the flesh of another. It was considered a mental illness.

FEAR: Now the director in you comes out. Calling yourself mentally ill is classic overdramatization. A person of your wealth is not mentally ill.

TRUTH: And what is the definition of mental illness?

FEAR: There are many forms of mental illness. I cannot limit it to one answer.

TRUTH: But there is a baseline definition. A common perception shared by all of the mentally ill. Do you know what this is?

FEAR: I know what the textbooks say. A mentally ill person operates outside of reality, outside the bounds of what is real.

TRUTH: Yes. A mentally ill person does not see things as they are. And if it is true, as the mystics state, that everything is connected—that reality at its most fundamental is one, that we are all brothers and sisters, that I am connected to all of creation—can you not see that by keeping so much while others went without, by consuming resources without regard, I was operating outside the bounds of reality, and I was indeed mentally ill?

FEAR: You said *if* what the mystics state is true. I do not subscribe to the idealism of the mystics!

TRUTH: This will be examined in time. But for now, can you accept the premise that what the mystics have told us for millennia is true? And if true, does this not then make the term *mentally ill* applicable?

FEAR: Under your conditions, *if* the mystics are correct, yes, the term is applicable.

TRUTH: And why is it applicable?

FEAR: Must I say it?

(A long pause.)

FEAR: Okay, fine. If everything is one, by keeping so much while others have so little, you are only hurting yourself. When others suffer, you suffer. I get it. But isn't your use of the term inappropriate? Isn't it disrespectful to call yourself mentally ill when others are suffering from actual mental illness?

TRUTH: I do not say it with the slightest sense of irony. If my mind-set contributed to the suffering of others, this is an illness of the highest order.

FEAR: If this is an illness, as you say, then it is rampant.

TRUTH: It is indeed rampant. It is a worldwide epidemic.

FEAR: Then it is further proof that mankind is defective and flawed. How else could we get so off course?

TRUTH: Your question is valid and worthy of consideration. Shall we ask it?

INCEPTION

✳

Society everywhere is in conspiracy against the
manhood of every one of its members.

—RALPH WALDO EMERSON

WHAT IF I TOLD YOU that you are more than likely asleep. And
by asleep, I mean that your thoughts may not be your own, that
you are in all probability under the influence, even under the
control, of someone else. In Christopher Nolan's science fiction
thriller, *Inception,* that's the basic premise; that it's possible
to enter a person's mind, plant an idea, and then make the
individual think that the newly planted idea is his or her own.
As futuristic and fantastic as this sounds, consider that this may
not be science fiction at all; this may be what is happening to
you and me and to most members of our culture, unaware.

Never before in history have human beings become subject to
so many sources of influence. With the touch of a button, images
from around the world instantly appear on our computer screens,
our televisions, even our phones. And with that communication
come messages that beg our attention, demand our allegiance,
and not so subtly ask us to acquiesce. Whether we are pumping
gas, in line at the grocery store, checking e-mails, watching
TV, reading a magazine, strolling city streets, or traveling in
an airplane, someone is selling something, pushing a product,
a promise, a lifestyle. And the theme that undergirds these
messages is clear. We are told not that we already *are* someone,

beautiful in the eyes of a loving Creator, but that we have to *be* someone. *"Here's what success looks like! It wears a suit and a tie and comes with a certain income, job status, and body type." "You need the latest iPad and iPhone, and as soon as we invent an iCar, you'll need that, too!" "And don't forget, take care of yourself first, be number one, and above all, win!"* The message is transparent and telling: as currently constituted, we do not measure up.

Twentieth-century mystic Thomas Merton saw firsthand this insidious influence and believed it leads to the formation of a *false self*, drawing us away from authenticity into the control and expectations of others. Consider the word *authenticity*— it is rooted in the same word as *author*, so when we are inauthentic, in one sense, we are not the authors of our own lives; someone or something is writing our story. This can have devastating consequences, dousing the flame of the human spirit, snuffing out an individual's life-giving spark. You only have to look at today's soaring statistics on suicide, depression, and mood-altering medications to see how many people have lost passion and purpose. Listen to the lament of mystic poet Rainer Maria Rilke:

No one lives his life.

Disguised since childhood,
haphazardly assembled
from voices and fears and little pleasures,
we come of age as masks.

Our true face never speaks.

Somewhere there must be storehouses
where all these lives are laid away
like suits of armor or old carriages
or clothes hanging limply on the walls.

Maybe all paths lead there,
to the repository of unlived things.

Ancient wisdom and our spiritual traditions ask something quite different: *"To be full, you must first be empty." "Be still and know that I am God."* But modern society has inverted this wisdom, keeping us satiated and in constant motion. The voice of God, our own Highest Voice, becomes crowded out in the process, paving the way for the ultimate tragedy—we mistake the societal voice as our own.

How did these social pressures arise that mask our own true voice? Is this just who we human beings are, dense and dumb herd animals, easily swayed to follow the collective? What will it take to break out of this pack mentality and burst into the light of authenticity?

Dialogue Five:

FEAR: *Inception* was a popular film, but it will not make a popular philosophy. You are really convinced that people are asleep?
TRUTH: I am convinced that few people live their own lives, yes.

FEAR: You have seen too many movies.
TRUTH: I have seen society.

FEAR: So society is the culprit?

TRUTH: To point to society is to give power to what exists on the outside. Society is simply the collective energy of the individuals that make up that society. The individual must take responsibility for his own voice. *"And where is the power of error? We find it was after all, not in the city, but in ourselves."*

FEAR: Do you really expect an individual to stand up to society? It is only natural that he follows the masses. They are thousands, he is one.

TRUTH: And in that one is great power. The power to change the thousands.

FEAR: Once again, you are being unrealistic. What is any single person supposed to do in the midst of the crowd? How can he ever hope to turn that crowd around?

TRUTH: An individual is not responsible for the crowd, only for his reaction to the crowd. Will he allow it to suppress his own true voice? Or will he have the courage to forge his own path? In the end, if he allows himself to succumb to the roar of the societal monster and is absorbed by that monster, he himself becomes a part of the beast that rampages on.

FEAR: But what do you mean, people do not live their own lives? People have choices. We live in a free society.

TRUTH: Just because a person is not in jail does not make him free. Many in prison are free, and many walking free are imprisoned.

FEAR: But we are the envy of the world. Our society is known for its freedom.

TRUTH: Almost one in four of our children goes to bed hungry. Are they free? Fifty percent of our college students have contemplated suicide. Are they free? We leave our parents to die in nursing homes. Are they free?

FEAR: There are problems in every society. It is not a matter of freedom.

TRUTH: When a child believes he must win to be worthy, when young adults define themselves by what they do and not who they are, it is a kind of slavery a slave master would envy.

FEAR: And what is wrong with winning? What is wrong with identifying yourself by what you do? People *are* what they do.

TRUTH: And when they are doing nothing, what are they? They are people who feel like nothing. The kingdom of heaven resides inside them, and they are distraught over a pause in their paycheck.

FEAR: There is nothing wrong with taking pride in what you do, in being able to make it on your own.

TRUTH: Ah yes, rugged independence. An idea that conquered the West but did not conquer what needs to be conquered.

(*Truth looks right at Fear . . .*)

FEAR: What? *I* need to be conquered? I am good for people. I keep them focused on what is ahead. On their future.
TRUTH: Which the prophets have duly warned against.

FEAR: The prophets were all dreamers. Like the Galilean, Jesus. *"Do not worry about tomorrow . . ."* Ha! If we do not worry about tomorrow, who will?
TRUTH: And why is it tomorrow cannot be considered without worry?

FEAR: Because without worry, people become lazy. Give them a healthy dose of it, a healthy dose of me, and they wake up.
TRUTH: Worry has little to do with waking up. It has little to do with anything of value. Yes, entire industries have been created in homage to worry: auto insurance, health insurance, life insurance, 401(k)s, retirement accounts. But do you not see what all of this is? It is making yourself sick in order to lay up something for a sick day. It is you, Fear, trying to control what cannot be controlled. And what is it you want to control so desperately?

FEAR: Don't say it! I do not want to have this conversation!
TRUTH: Yes, you do all you can to ensure that we never face it. You make sure we are embalmed, expressions frozen in place, our bodies laid in sealed boxes where the worms cannot eat us. All to preserve the illusion of our physical immortality. Do you not see, Fear, that death is a part of life. It will always be so. And when you accept this, the natural cycle of which we are all a part, then perhaps the 401(k), the retirement account, insurance on top of insurance, can be used to meet today's need rather than

tomorrow's fear. As Jesus said, *"For tomorrow has enough troubles of its own."*

FEAR: *"And who among you by worrying can add a single hour to his life?!"* Blah, blah, blah! It won't stop me from trying.
TRUTH: And with so much trying, do you not see that you become tried? Do you not see how much is provided without your own effort, without worry? For nine months, a fertilized egg grows perfectly in a womb. Is this due to worry? The blood flows freely in your veins sustaining life in all reaches of the body. Is this thanks to worry? The sun rises each morning and takes its life-giving arc across the sky, all without worry. If you could see, Fear, how much has been provided without your conscious concern, you would take the prophet at his word when he said to not even store into barns. You might, just might, begin to rest like the lilies of the field and the birds of the air.

FEAR: People are not birds and they are not lilies! And people cannot rest! Or else . . .

(Fear hesitates.)

TRUTH: Or else what?

FEAR: Or they might die!
TRUTH: Yes, it's possible. People might die. But something else is also possible, and even likely. They just might begin to live. To really live.

OUR CULTURAL STORY

✳

*As human beings, our greatness lies in not
so much being able to remake the world
—that is the myth of the atomic age—
as in being able to remake ourselves.*

—MAHATMA GANDHI

*We should split the sack
of this culture
And stick our heads out.*

—RUMI

I WAS RAISED IN THE CATHOLIC FAITH, and like all good Catholics, I was taught that, well, Catholics aren't good. In fact, no one is. Each of us, tall and short, white and black, Jew and Gentile, is born bad. That's right, all of humanity is defective, emerging from the womb with a decidedly depraved and sinful nature. This is why we choose greed over good, and selfish gain over serving others. This is why we're inauthentic, why a destructive societal hum emerges—bad individuals put out bad messages, which further poison already bad people. This negative story isn't just confined to the religious. The vast majority outside the faith perspective subscribe to a similar notion that man's basic nature is aggressive, greedy, and competitive; it's why we have so many wars, why we're destroying the environment, and why the gap continues to grow between the rich and poor. Society's so screwed up because we're so screwed up. But what if this story about our inherent defects is just that, *a story*? What if we are actually good in our nature, divinely designed so, hardwired to help and to love?

I first woke up to this possibility a few years ago, when I asked a question that would change the course of my life. Morgan Freeman and I had become friends on the set of *Bruce Almighty*, and when production wrapped, we went out to dinner. Here's the question that lead me down a path that would eventually rock my universe: *"Morgan, we put words in your mouth as God. Tell me, what do you believe?"*

He quickly measured my resolve, and when I didn't back down he said, *"Have you ever heard of the tyranny of agriculture, son?"*

I stumbled through some generic answer, and Morgan being, well, God, knew I was off track and suggested I read *Ishmael* by Daniel Quinn, with the promise that we would talk again.

There are books you can't put down and others that won't put you down. *Ishmael* was the latter, grabbing me by my throat in a literary vise grip. Quinn's chokehold is rooted in a simple idea: that our culture has seduced us, hypnotized us really, into wholeheartedly embracing a way of life that may have little to do with reality. Like in the movie *Inception,* or Thomas Merton's notion of the false self, it may have planted ideas in our head and made us think those ideas are our own. Quinn calls this underlying influence our *cultural story,* which is defined as *a set of beliefs or principles that guide the behavior of a particular culture.* Little did I know until that fateful reading of *Ishmael,* that I had become the product of a cultural story, behaving as

I was taught, convinced I was doing good, all the while adding my share to the collective insanity.

So what exactly is our cultural story? What is the accepted ideology that shaped my life, that led me into hypocritical behaviors, unaware? I've broken it down into three basic tenets:

1. *Mankind is separate from nature, born with the right to conquer and rule the natural world.*
2. *Man is separate from his fellow man.*
3. *Human nature is flawed; human beings are born aggressive, selfish, sinful, and bad.*

The first tenet is so widely accepted it requires little explanation. We see its manifestation everywhere. Mankind simply, and with certainty, regards itself as the most important species on the planet. Our religions wholeheartedly endorse this idea with the creation story in Genesis chapters one and two, stating in no uncertain terms that humans have been given dominion to rule over all life. Simply put, the entire world was made for man. The world wasn't made for anteaters or aardvarks, slugs or slime; it was made for humans, and with this entitlement comes the right to do to nature as we please.

Once man separated himself from nature, the groundwork was laid for humans to see themselves as separate from each other. Charles Darwin articulates the reasoning for this separation when he writes that mankind is locked in a competitive struggle, and individuals must look out for themselves in a never-ending battle of *"survival of the fittest."* (This of course, is a widely held *misinterpretation* of Darwin. More on this later.) Newtonian science further supports this idea theorizing that we live in a predictable and reliable universe where *separate objects* act according to fixed laws in time and space. The key idea here is that objects, including people, are *separate;* to affect a person, you have to do something physical to him, like poke, prod, or push him.

The final tenet, the belief that human nature is flawed, comes from both religion and science, which have long held man to be aggressive and violent in nature. In the Judeo-Christian faith, for example, human beings are born into a condition known as *original sin.* Because Eve ate of the forbidden fruit, the entire human race became corrupted and cursed. A similar story about the "fall" of man can be found in other faiths, from Islam to Buddhism, Hinduism to Zoroastrianism.

Once I woke up to this ideological overlay, I began to see it everywhere: in television shows, in advertisements, in church sermons, on the Internet, in daily conversations. Here's a sample of what I heard regarding the invented chatter we take for granted as fact: *"Separate yourself from the pack," "Be number one," "Compete and win," "Accumulate wealth," "To the victor belong the spoils," "Our nation is the greatest," "A penny saved is a penny earned," "Bigger is better," "Be somebody or be gone," "Growth is good," "College is the best four years of your life," "Technology equals progress," "You can have it all," "Time is money,"* and so on and so forth. And if it weren't clear enough that we were being fed a specific agenda, I took another look at the term *culture* and saw it rooted in a very telling word: *cult!*

---

* Author's note: For a more in-depth examination of our cultural story, see Thom Hartmann's *Last Hours of Ancient Sunlight;* Daniel Quinn's trilogy, *Ishmael, The Story of B,* and *My Ishmael;* and Riane Eisler's *The Chalice and the Blade.*

Dialogue Six:

FEAR: Once again, you are making a big deal out of nothing, seeing ghosts and shadows where there are none.

TRUTH: Your comment, Fear, is precisely why cultural stories have power. Most people do not know they even exist. It's really all a matter of perspective. If, for example, you stood close to a mosaic, say just a few inches away, you would see individual stones or gems, but the full picture wouldn't emerge until you took a step back. To see the whole picture requires a change of perspective. That's also true of our cultural story; we need to take a step back to get a full view of what has been in front of us all along.

FEAR: Suppose this is true. Suppose our society is telling a story. Isn't that what societies are supposed to do? Choose what they value and promote those things?

TRUTH: Of course. But the relevant question is not *is a culture telling a story?* but *is the story the culture's telling true?*

FEAR: But you have just told the American cultural story. What about other cultural stories? Germany, Japan, China, Russia? This inquiry seems endless!

TRUTH: The inquiry is not endless. In fact, there have only been two cultural stories in the 175,000-year history of man. China, Russia, Germany, and Japan—all are inside the same cultural story.

FEAR: What? China is communist! Russia, for centuries, was socialist! These are different stories!

TRUTH: The story may play itself out differently, but the underpinnings are the same.

FEAR: So you would equate democracy with communism? A republic with a dictatorship? This is ignorance!

TRUTH: You are looking only at the surface of a society. Look beneath.

FEAR: What do you mean, look beneath? How?

TRUTH: Do you recall the three basic tenets of our cultural story?

FEAR: Of course. You said we see ourselves as separate from nature and each other, and we believe mankind's nature is flawed. So?

TRUTH: So now consider communist China. Do they believe man is separate from nature? That man is superior to nature?

FEAR: How should I know? I'm not communist, and I'm not Chinese.

TRUTH: Simple observation will provide the answer. How do they treat nature? Do they pollute?

FEAR: Every industrialized nation pollutes.

TRUTH: And what mentality allows these nations to do this? Do they believe they are one with nature or separate from it?

FEAR: They see nature like we do, as something to be subdued, as something to be conquered.

TRUTH: In other words, they see nature as separate . . . And what is China's view of man? Do they consider themselves connected to all mankind, or separate? What has their history taught you?

FEAR: They protect their borders with ferocity.

TRUTH: Precisely. They've killed thousands, if not millions, to do so.

FEAR: But they do protect their own people. What about that?

TRUTH: Let's look at their own people. Do they view their citizens as basically good, worthy of freedom and self-expression?

FEAR: Of course not. They're communist! The government controls the population with an iron fist.

TRUTH: Controls them from what? What is the government protecting the people from?

(Fear hesitates.)

FEAR: From themselves. From their own ignorance; from their own greed and selfishness.

TRUTH: So China, even though it is communist, still views its people as defective and flawed. And if we were to ask these questions of the former Soviet Union or the Japanese Empire, would we not get the same answers? Did they not dominate nature, have enemies the world over, and see their populations as flawed and in need of control?

FEAR: Okay, fine. You've made your point. But why does any of this really matter? What good will it do to know that our culture is telling a story, a story of separation?

TRUTH: As Frederick Nietzsche believed, if you can understand the *why*, you can endure any *how*. So, if we want to know *how* to change our world, we must first understand the *why*; why our world is broken . . . Our cultural story is the why.

FEAR: Our culture may be telling a story, but it is not why the world is broken. The world is broken because it is what it is, *dog eat dog.*

TRUTH: I see.

(A long pause.)

FEAR: What?

TRUTH: It's interesting, that's all. That this is what we now believe, that the world is dog eat dog. And we base our society on such a saying.

FEAR: And what is wrong with that?

TRUTH: I have never seen a dog eat another dog, have you?

DIVIDING GOD

✳

The reason why the world lacks unity,
and lies broken and in heaps,
is because man is disunited with himself.
—RALPH WALDO EMERSON

WHEN PREPARING TO FILM THE DOCUMENTARY *I AM*, I told a friend I planned on asking two questions: *What's wrong with the world?* and *What can we do about it?* She responded, *"Wow. That's going to be one long documentary!"* With all due respect to my friend, I see things differently. War, genocide, greed, economic inequity, the environmental crisis, racism, slavery, bullying, school shootings, high murder and crime rates, high rates of depression and suicide—virtually all are traceable to a single, simple root cause; a root cause that has disconnected mankind from nature, reality, himself. This root cause is the story we are now telling ourselves: the story that we are competitive and corrupt; that we are not brothers and sisters; that we are not one with all of creation. Consider this: the word *devil* in Greek etymology, is rooted in the word, *diabollein,* meaning to tear apart, or to divide. So the devil,* beyond any ideas of good and evil, is the force that separates, that divides. In direct contrast, God, according to the mystical

---

* Author's note: The term *devil* is not meant to refer to a physical being or to invoke mythological images of a man in a red suit with horns, a pointed tail, and a pitchfork. Here it simply refers to the idea or the energy that pushes us apart, that disunites.

traditions, unites; God is indivisible; God is one. Thus, the poet Hafiz wisely observed, *we have exhausted ourselves dividing God all day, and thus need rest.*

Of course, politicians, the media, and a host of institutions advocate a very different message; that complicated factors have created the crises of the day. But like a body manifesting multiple symptoms—fever, chills, dizziness, upset stomach, sallow skin tone, vomiting—all of which result from a single poison ingested, so, too, the world's symptoms are the result of ingesting a single toxic ideology. And if this is indeed true, then the most incredible idea isn't this singular causal theory of separation, it's this: if we can identify the cause of the world's illness, can we not identify the antidote, as well?

Dialogue Seven:

FEAR: Your separatist ideology is, once again, far too simplistic. People themselves are complicated, so the problems they create are complicated, as well.
TRUTH: Solving these problems will involve complicated actions, yes, complex programs, certainly. But the *cause* of these problems is not complicated.

FEAR: Generalities won't win me over, or anyone for that matter. Can you not be more specific? Or is it that you have no specifics to offer?
TRUTH: Let me first ask a question: Why are the vast majority of children raised in loving families so well taken care of? Why do

they have enough food to eat, adequate shelter, medicine, clothes, even the resources to get an education?

FEAR: It's obvious why. Because they have a family to look after them!

TRUTH: Why don't these families charge each other for food, for shelter? Why don't parents try to make a profit off of their children say, when they get sick?

FEAR: Now you're being ridiculous. You're not going to charge someone in your family if they're sick!

TRUTH: So it's unthinkable to make a profit off of a son or daughter, especially when they're down. What about a relative, like a brother or an uncle or a cousin?

FEAR: It's the same. Most people aren't going to make a buck off of their relatives.

TRUTH: What about a close friend or a neighbor? Is it okay to make a profit off of them?

FEAR: I don't know. What's your point with all of this?

TRUTH: My point is this: where does your family end and those you can take advantage of, those from whom you can extract a profit, begin?

FEAR: Are you saying the world's problems are caused by people seeking to make a profit off each other?

TRUTH: The world's problems are caused by the *mentality* that allows people to make a profit off each other.

FEAR: Scientists, philosophers, and politicians have debated this question—what causes the world's ills—for centuries. Virtually none have offered the naïve explanation that the world's problems boil down to a single fact.

TRUTH: And yet no scientist today would debate that a single germ could wipe out all human life on the planet. Why then is it so naïve to believe a single toxic ideology could do the same? List the world's problems and you will find the same theme running underneath. Why was Africa exploited for her resources? Did Westerners see Africans as family members or separate? What about Haiti when she was turned into a slave colony? Was she populated with extended family to be nurtured or laborers to be exploited? What about slaves themselves—today's slaves and yesterday's, as well—are they family members or just another means to achieve self-seeking ends? What about the homeless in need of medical care? What about a child who is bullied or even a river that is polluted? Do you not see, Fear, that all of these toxic branches of the human story grow out of a single contaminated root?

FEAR: The toxic root is man himself. The ideology you speak of is born from the rotten root of man's corrupt nature.

TRUTH: If this is true, then why, for most of man's history, did he tell a very different story?

FEAR: You have said this before, that mankind has told a different story. What is this story?

TRUTH: This is our next topic, the only other cultural story the human species has ever told. Who lived this story? And what makes it so radically different from our current view of the world?

THE INDIGENOUS STORY

✳

*The ancients knew something that
we seem to have forgotten.*

—ALBERT EINSTEIN

IT WAS SHOCKING enough to discover that our culture was telling a story, but it was even more shocking to discover that our cultural story is so young, only 10,000 years old, first surfacing when man invented agriculture. Thus, incredibly, our current cultural story represents only a tiny fraction of human history, less than 6 percent of all of the time mankind has walked on earth. For 165,000 years, or 94 percent of our history, humans lived under a radically different collective story, which we will call *the native,* or *indigenous, story.* That story goes like this:

Mankind is a part of the natural world and is utterly dependent upon it for his survival. He is not separate from nature, but is connected to it, to the earth, and all living things.

Let's be clear—this is not to promote the idea of the noble savage. Native cultures engaged in many behaviors we would not want to emulate. And there were certainly drawbacks and limits to their way of life that the current cultural story has allowed us to move beyond, with medical, technological, and scientific advances. But it's hard to ignore the fact that their basic philosophy did allow humanity to live sustainably for tens of thousands of years. For example:

- For the vast majority of our history, humans lived in relatively simple housing—in tents, huts, or modest dwellings. Structures, by and large, were egalitarian, arrayed in communal villages. Today's cultural story gave rise to great disparities in housing—from mud huts to mansions—with fences, walls, and gates erected in between.

- The emphasis of indigenous society was the group; tasks were routinely shared, promoting interaction between tribal members, with communal gatherings arising as an organic part of daily life. The current cultural story stresses the individual over the group, with occupational specialization dividing up once communal tasks, further isolating people from one another.

- Native populations did engage in conflicts, mostly over territory and resources, but the resulting violence was almost always small-scale and limited. Neighboring tribes were seen as essential for trading and as potential candidates for intermarriage to diversify the gene pool. Widespread war and genocide, all too common today, were virtually unheard of.

- Finally, for tens of thousands of years, humans left the natural landscape relatively unaltered. The current cultural vision gave rise to industrial waste, toxic runoff, clear-cutting, mountaintop removal, poisonous mining practices, and widespread pollution.

So, what happened? How did humans go from the indigenous, sustainable philosophy to one that soon may end life as we know it? What led to the suppression of one story and the explosion of another?

Dialogue Eight:

FEAR: You say you are not calling natives noble, but it's clear you are doing exactly that.

TRUTH: Labeling native philosophy noble or naïve is not my intention. I only wish to reflect the principles that the vast majority of native cultures embraced. These cultures had tens of thousands of years to test the laws of life and the way things work. Their philosophies simply represent the wisdom garnered from this long period of trial and error.

FEAR: But you believe their philosophy is better than the current mind-set, do you not?

TRUTH: This is not a question of better or worse. This is an attempt to identify the principles on which the human race can move forward.

FEAR: Then why do you hold Chief Seattle and his letter in such high regard? Admit it, you put him on a pedestal.

TRUTH: His words have power. His words ring true. Let the reader decide:

Excerpts of a letter from Chief Seattle to the United States government, 1800:

"The President in Washington sends word that he wishes to buy our land.

Buy our land? But how can you buy or sell the sky? the land? The idea is strange to us. If we do not own the freshness of the air and the sparkle of the water, how can you buy them?

Every part of this earth is sacred to my people. Every shining pine needle, every sandy shore, every mist in the dark woods, every meadow, every humming insect. All are holy in the memory and experience of my people . . .

This we know. The earth does not belong to man; man belongs to the earth. All things are connected like the blood that unites one family . . .

Man did not weave the web of life, he is merely a strand in it. Whatever he does to the web, he does to himself . . .

No man, be he red man or white man, can be apart.

One thing we know: There is only one God. We are all brothers."

FEAR: This is unfair. No one can even confirm this letter is authentic, that it was even a part of history.

TRUTH: You, Fear, are under the mistaken notion that a story has to have happened to be true. *Alice in Wonderland* did not happen and it is filled with truth. So, too, are *1984, Crime and Punishment, The Alchemist,* and countless other works of fiction. Chief Seattle's letter is representative of native philosophy. Of this, there is no debate.

FEAR: But no single speech can speak for all tribes. No single articulation represents all indigenous people.

TRUTH: If a modern day president speaks of winning, of being number one, of national pride, could you tell me what country he is speaking from?

FEAR: Of course not. It could be from any number of countries.

TRUTH: Why?

FEAR: Because most countries have points of national pride, most countries like to win, most countries wish to be number one.

TRUTH: Because most modern-day nations are all inside the same cultural story. The story of separation. The same is true of the indigenous story. Most share a belief that the earth is sacred, that the rivers, trees, oceans, and air provide life and sustenance; most share the knowledge that all things are connected and are one.

FEAR: But once again, you point out the negative side of our story. The story of competition, of being number one, of pride.

TRUTH: This is not meant to be negative or positive. Both stories have advantages. Both have consequences.

FEAR: But the current cultural story has overtaken the indigenous story. It has won out. Doesn't that imply that it's superior?

TRUTH: And what do you mean by superior?

FEAR: If what you say is true, if the current story is only 10,000 years old, then within that same time span, within just 5.7 percent of human history, it has taken over the entire earth. If the current cultural story is simply not better, what allowed this to happen so quickly?

TRUTH: Do you recall Jesus' warning in Matthew 6:26 about *storing into barns?*

FEAR: Yes. I have never understood this warning.

TRUTH: What allows a culture to store into barns?

FEAR: What do you mean, allows a culture to store into barns?

TRUTH: For 165,000 years, man was a hunter and gatherer. Always foraging, always on the move. Suddenly, he becomes an accumulator. What happened?

FEAR: And what is wrong with accumulation? Accumulating things, storing things is just common sense.

TRUTH: It is indeed common today. Only time will tell if it made sense.

FEAR: Of course it makes sense! You can save something for a rainy day.

TRUTH: And if by saving something for a rainy day, you poison the rain itself—this makes sense? For the vast majority of history, man did not accumulate or store into barns. But something happened to change that, and in turn, it changed the course of human history.

FEAR: So what happened?
TRUTH: Agriculture happened.

THE TYRANNY OF AGRICULTURE

✳

Consider the birds of the air; they do not
sew nor reap, nor gather into barns,
yet your heavenly Father feeds them.

—MATTHEW 6:26

Do not worry about tomorrow,
for tomorrow has enough cares of its own.

—MATTHEW 6:34

IN THE DOCUMENTARY *I AM,* I declare myself to have been mentally ill. Now this sounds like a joke setup, but unfortunately, I wasn't joking. The amount of resources I used, the material goods I accumulated, were far out of proportion with what I needed for my own personal happiness and contentment. It was a way of life, the very model of success I had learned from my culture, a way of walking in the world that I accepted as good and right. The indigenous populations that once inhabited North America believed the opposite—that excessive materialism was an illness. They held that those who take more than they need suffer from a false perspective, a perspective that disconnects them from the earth that sustains them and from the human family of which they are a part. They first saw this mentality among the European settlers who arrived on their shores, plundering nature and the native people they found there. So where did this mentality originate, this illness that has little regard for anything outside of personal gain? Interestingly, it began with the most innocent of discoveries. That discovery is agriculture.

Wait a second—agriculture? That purest of pastimes, the growing and harvesting of food, led to a worldwide epidemic of excess, violence, overconsumption, and greed? Yes. You see, conceptually, agriculture may seem innocent enough and allow for the conveniences of modern society, but the shift in the way mankind viewed the world was anything but innocent. You will recall that for the first 165,000 years of man's history, humans lived as hunter-gatherers, in tribes of roughly 30 to 150. In these cultures, food was sought on a daily basis; if the tribe found no game or food, they did not eat. As we have seen, this bred a deep interdependence among indigenous populations, an inherent respect for the group and for nature. If the natural world did not provide, the tribe would die; if tribal members did not find food, they would cease to exist. When agriculture arrives on the scene, man is given the opportunity to radically shift not only his outcome—whether he lives or dies—but his attitude. He is no longer limited by what nature provides but can now create his own provisions by *conquering and controlling* nature. Thus, large areas, even entire forests, are cleared to grow food, food that can now be stored. Water is diverted to irrigate fields, disrupting the natural flow of rivers and streams. Nutritional needs can now be handled by a few tribesmen, leaving others time to focus on varying tasks—some weave baskets, some build huts, others craft tools and refine weapons. Thus, *specialization emerges,* as tasks once shared by the group are divided up, separating people from organic communal ties. For the first time in history, individuals are told they have to *earn a living*, as societies begin to lock up food and distribute that food only to those whose work is seen as valuable. Envy ripens among tribal members, leaving some to wonder why others have more than they need. Competition increases among once cooperating neighbors. And with an abundant food supply comes a consequence that has dire implications for man's ability to survive: *population rapidly increases*. Remember Morgan Freeman's *tyranny of agriculture?* This is it: *mankind can now produce through synthetics enough food to sustain a population that cannot presently sustain the earth.*

Dialogue Nine:

FEAR: So now what, you would have us all go back to living as hunter-gatherers? To foraging for food?
TRUTH: No one is suggesting we abandon agriculture.

FEAR: But are you not implying agriculture is evil? That it is destroying our world?
TRUTH: I am implying nothing of the sort. Agriculture is not evil, and it is not destroying our world. Agriculture is a tool. Neither good nor bad. It is the mind-set that moves the tool that must be called into question, a mind-set that absorbed or killed off most who did not subscribe to its ways.

FEAR: Isn't that just more proof that mankind is inherently flawed? He comes up with a new tool and look what he does with it—destroys everything!

TRUTH: Mankind is not flawed, he is young. Put a knife in the hand of a surgeon and lives will be saved. Put that same knife in the hands of a child and blood will be spilled. We are that child. We are a young species, and we are now spilling blood with a tool that can save lives.

FEAR: Why do you say we are young? You said we are 175,000 years old. That's ancient!

TRUTH: On an evolutionary scale it is adolescence. Life on this planet began 4 billion years ago. In the skies, 13 billion years ago. It took time for life, for nature to achieve balance. And it will take time for us, as well.

FEAR: You say it is a matter of time. I say it is a matter of answering your original question, who are we? And who we are is a flawed species prone to aggressive and selfish behaviors. Mankind is bent on his own destruction. He has always been this way and will always be this way.

TRUTH: If this is true, that mankind is basically flawed, it would be natural for the world to be the way it is, with widespread war, poverty, and strife. Man is broken, and so he creates a broken world. This is your contention?

FEAR: Yes. Man is who he is and you can expect no better of him. As I said, why else would the current mind-set win out if it isn't who we are?

TRUTH: The relevant question isn't, *why did one mind-set win and one lose?* The question that needs to be asked is, *which mind-set is true?*

FEAR: I know what is true. I see it on the news every day: murder, crime, environmental destruction, struggle, strife, division, death.

TRUTH: And if it can be demonstrated that the opposite is true, what then?

FEAR: And how exactly will you do that? How exactly will you determine what is real, what is true?

TRUTH: To determine what is true in life, what is written inside life's operating manual, would we not look at life, at all of life: human beings, nature, biology, and the subatomic world? Is it not time to ask the question?

FEAR: What question is this?

TRUTH: The question that supersedes all other questions: *How does life work?*

SPOOKY ACTION

✳

Not on my authority, but on that of truth,
it is wise for you to accept the fact
that all things are one.

—HERACLITUS 500 BC

AT THE TURN OF THE 20TH CENTURY, a new field of inquiry emerged known as quantum mechanics or quantum physics that would turn the scientific world upside down. Quantum physics is essentially the science of the small, the subatomic, the tiny stuff of which we are all made. What scientists found there in the infinitesimal has them rethinking not only hundreds of years of research, but also the basic nature of reality, itself.

The notion that first caught their attention is known as *quantum entanglement.* (If you are new to this phenomenon, hang on to your head because it might just get blown off.) Entanglement is all about interconnectivity, about the unbreakable bond between particles at the subatomic level. The theory states that if two electrons that are in relationship with each other (entangled) are *separated up to an infinite distance,* when the rotation of one electron is manipulated or affected, the rotation of the other electron is affected *simultaneously.* The key idea to note here is that the effect happens simultaneously; the instant the initial particle is affected, the distant particle is affected, as well. To put this on a human scale, imagine two bowling balls "entangled" in Los Angeles. If we were to separate those two bowling balls by flying one halfway around the world to Shanghai, when we affect the spin of the bowling ball in Los Angeles, the spin of the bowling ball in Shanghai becomes affected at exactly the same time!

This phenomenon was initially so strange and off-putting that Einstein called it *"spooky action at a distance."* But the more scientists looked into this phenomenon, the more it held up to their scrutiny. In fact, entanglement theory is no longer considered theory; what started out as spooky action is now accepted science. The implications are staggering. If you recall, Newtonian science posits that objects are *separate,* and to affect one, you have to poke it, prod it, or push it. But with quantum entanglement, nothing, *no-thing,* is apparently pushing or prodding a distant electron, and yet, the distant electron is affected all the same. This has been called the most profound discovery in all of physics because it proves that our accepted understanding of the fundamental nature of reality has been wrong; that all of life is not separate, but connected.

✳

THERE IS MORE to this quantum world, including an enigma known as *the double slit experiment.* For this experiment, researchers shoot electrons through one of two slits and then note the behavior of those electrons *after* they've traveled through those slits. (To do this, scientists set up a wall behind the slit through which the electrons will be shot. Then, *after the experiment is over*, they take note of the pattern the electrons leave on the wall.) Here's what's mind-blowing: Electrons behave one way until researchers introduce a device that "watches" or records the movement of the electrons. Once the recording device is introduced, the electrons behave in a *completely different way*. Just the act of observation somehow changes the way the electrons move through the slits—as if these electrons know they are being observed!

✳

FURTHERMORE, WHEN SCIENTISTS examine the smallest known particles in the universe, they find that these particles are often not particles at all, but vary between two states: the state of being a *set something* (a particle), and *a vibrating packet of energy* (a wave). Thus, at the very base of life, there is a constant pulsating dance—particles are always shifting into waves, and waves are shifting back into particles. And just like the double slit experiment, what makes a wave lock into its particle form is *when you look at it!* That's right, *observation* or *consciousness* appears to be what transforms energy/waves into the stuff that we call matter and life.

✳

IF YOU HAVEN'T yet cued the *Twilight Zone* music, there's more. The deeper scientists probe into the world of the small, they observe that no object has any end or edge to it—that nothing is really solid. And so, if you were to look at my hand at the subatomic level, you would only see subatomic particles floating in space; in other words, there would be *no end to me and no beginning of you*. "My" subatomic particles are constantly mixing with the subatomic particles of "the air," which further mix with the subatomic particles of "you." All matter, in fact, is intermingling all the time. Moreover, the space between things, which was once assumed to be empty, is not empty at all. Scientists have discovered a *connective web of energy* that inhabits all space. It is this fabric of energy that could explain why entangled particles remain connected across infinite distances—a web of energy, or a field, may be holding these particles together, in connection, regardless of the distance between them.

In sum, the recent findings in quantum physics point to one consistent conclusion: *The very basic nature of life is connection. Nothing is separate. In fact, everything may be connected everywhere at all times.*

✻

ALTERNATIVE SCIENCE IS also pushing the bounds of accepted reality. Here are just a few examples of recent, potentially groundbreaking studies that test the principles of "spooky action" in our everyday world:

- Rupert Sheldrake is well known for his decade-long studies of connectivity, such as his famous experiment asking the question, *"When does your dog know you're coming home?"* We all know our animals meet us at the door when we return home. The question is, when does the dog initially move to the door? Is it when the animal hears the car pull in the driveway or when the key hits the door? Sheldrake set up cameras in multiple houses and found convincing statistical evidence that the dog moves to the door *when its owner makes the decision to come home!* That's right, when the owner *decides* to come home—whether from across the street or across town—somehow the dog registers the decision and moves to the door!

• The HeartMath Institute has repeatedly demonstrated that our moods not only affect other people but can affect the living systems around us. I participated in one such study known as the *Yogurt Experiment,* where a bowl of yogurt (a living system) was hooked up to a magnetometer. A magnetometer is a device designed to measure baseline energy levels—in this case, the energy emitted from the yogurt bacteria. I was then seated in front of the yogurt—I was not hooked up to the yogurt at all—and then asked to recall certain experiences that would elicit strong emotional responses, such as sadness or grief. Right on cue, as my emotional states changed, the needle on the magnetometer connected to the yogurt moved, as well. (This is documented in the film *I AM.*) Somehow, my emotional shifts and the energy of the yogurt acted in concert; when my emotions shifted, the yogurt's energy shifted simultaneously.

• *Separated DNA* is an experiment that has been replicated many times. Conventional science still cannot explain the results. Here's what happens: A test tube full of genetic material (DNA) is handed to a volunteer. This volunteer holds on to the test tube while listening to a story designed to produce a positive or negative emotion, like joy or rage. Let's suppose the feeling is positive, like joy. Impossibly, the genetic material in the glass expands and *moves toward* the person. If the feeling is rage, the DNA *shrinks away* from the person. Next, some of the DNA is then placed into a second test tube, and, while the volunteer stays in the first room with half of the DNA, a researcher takes the other half into a completely separate room. The same volunteer in the first room feels an emotion.

And here's where it gets even stranger: when the DNA in the first room expands or contracts, *so does the DNA in the next room.* The separated DNA follows the same emotional ups and downs *simultaneously* with the original DNA.

• *Entrainment studies,* or studies of *"entangled minds,"* have been performed for years with surprisingly consistent results. One of the first studies in 1965 reported that the EEGs of separated identical twins showed an inexplicable connection. When one twin was asked to close his or her eyes, which causes the brain's alpha rhythms to increase, the distant twin's alpha rhythms also increased. In a later entrainment study in 2003 using brain scanning technology (MRIs), a pair of related volunteers were placed in separate rooms. One volunteer was then asked to remain open to "receiving" the energy from his or her partner, and then his or her partner was asked to maintain the intention of "sending." A light was then flashed in the room of the sender. Incredibly, the visual cortex of the "receiving" person was stimulated when the distant, or "sending," partner was exposed to the flashing light!

THERE ARE MANY more studies demonstrating paradigm-shifting phenomena, including presentiment (the ability of the human heart to predict the future), remote viewing (the ability to mentally "send" the image of an object to a distant partner), and intuition. The evidence all leads to one consistent conclusion: *separation is an illusion, and the fundamental nature of reality is connection and unity.*

Dialogue Ten:

FEAR: There is so much to object to here, studies of dogs and yogurt. What does any of this have to do with the real world, the world of hunger and unpaid mortgages?

TRUTH: It suggests that hunger and unpaid mortgages are not separate from you. It suggests that when Martin Luther King, Jr. said that we are all *"tied in a single garment of destiny,"* he wasn't just talking morality, he was talking science.

FEAR: So somehow you are connecting my life to the life of the homeless man, to the plight of the hungry?

TRUTH: It is not a matter of connecting them, they are already connected.

FEAR: But other than quantum physics, everything you've mentioned is fringe science.

TRUTH: And what is wrong with fringe science? All science was once fringe science. The earth was once considered flat. Those who believed it was round were fringe scientists. Fringe science simply pushes at the edges of what is currently known. It is what all science is designed to do.

FEAR: But for every study you list, dozens of questions arise.

TRUTH: So ask them. There are questions about all new discoveries. But questions do not mean findings are false.

FEAR: But isn't all of this too new to be considered science? It is just theory for now and should be taken as such.
TRUTH: The phenomenon it explains is not new. Intuition, for example. The countless cases of information traveling instantaneously across space and time. The child who falls on the playground and the mother who instantly senses something is wrong. The twin on a flight over Europe whose body is racked with pain the precise moment her sibling is injured in a car accident in New York.

FEAR: It is chance, and chance alone, that explains these incidents. Every so often out of the millions of mothers in the world, one is going to imagine something has happened to her child at the precise moment it does.
TRUTH: Perhaps. But the statistics on such events have been calculated. The probability these are happening by chance is often tens of thousands, if not millions, to one.

FEAR: It is still a leap to believe these findings. The discoveries in quantum physics only apply to the microworld. And the examples you cite occur in the macroworld.
TRUTH: This is true. Most of the studies have been restricted to the subatomic world. But the dynamics between entangled particles and entangled minds are strikingly similar and cannot be easily dismissed.

FEAR: Still, not enough of this research has been scaled up, so I will remain a skeptic. Let science prove this beyond a doubt.
TRUTH: This is not all science has discovered to challenge our beliefs about who and what we are. There is more. Much more.

THE SCIENCE OF LOVE

✳

Admit something:
Everyone you see, you say to them, "Love me."
Of course, you do not say this out loud,
otherwise, someone would call the cops.
Still, though, think about this, this great
pull in us to connect.

—HAFIZ

FOR CENTURIES, IF NOT MILLENNIA, it has been widely accepted that human beings' basic nature is competitive, aggressive, and selfish, leaving many pessimistic about the future of mankind. But much of today's research in psychology, physiology, and sociology is not just challenging this assumption, but inverting it. The story now emerging from a wide range of disciplines is decidedly hopeful; that humans may actually be hardwired for good, and that our basic nature is empathetic, compassionate, and kind. For example:

• Would it surprise you to know that Charles Darwin used the phrase *survival of the fittest* only twice in *The Descent of Man* but used the word *love* 95 times? In fact, a closer look at Darwin reveals that he, too, glimpsed man's goodness. Thus, he notes it was mankind's ability to *cooperate* and *sympathize* that allowed this physically unremarkable species (we're relatively slow and weak compared to lions, great apes, tigers, and bears), in a relatively short amount of time, to grow from a tiny band of sub-Saharan nomads, to the most dominant species on the planet.

• In his seminal work, *The Empathic Civilization,* Jeremy Rifkin chronicles mankind's history from a very different perspective. It is not the history of a species hardwired for war, violence, aggression, and anger, but the opposite—a species wired for love, kindness, and compassion. *"Then why do acts of war, violence, and crime dominate our airwaves?"* one might ask. *"Why do we see them every night on TV?"* We are exposed to these acts, Rifkin believes, not because they are the norm of our species, but the exceptions. This is precisely why they are newsworthy; these negative, violent events are not reporting who we are, but who we are not!

• Rifkin's *Empathic Civilization* challenges us further, to think differently about human behavior, to look beyond the story we are presently being told. And what are we being told? That we are full of darkness; that it is every man for himself. And yet, how many countless acts of cooperation go unreported every day, every hour, every minute? How many greetings between people, how many doors opened, how many words of appreciation expressed, how many small acts of kindness performed, how many loving actions consummated, how many good-spirited conversations engaged in, how many gestures of generosity do not make the evening news? The number is incalculable. And yet, if one person steals a car, robs a bank, or injures another, this makes the headlines.

• Consider the simple act of driving to the grocery store. It, too, involves untold acts of cooperation: Drivers agree to stop at red lights, yield to oncoming traffic, drive within two lines, travel within certain speeds, slow at intersections, and signal for turns—not to mention the cooperative efforts undertaken to build roads, design vehicles, manufacture parts, and construct cars. Even sports teams brought together to compete only arrive at the playing field because multiple acts of cooperation got them there. Rifkin states his case with sound evidence compiled over the long course of human history: *The larger, unreported story of the human species is our desire to connect and cooperate, to give and receive love.*

✳

EVOLUTIONARY BIOLOGIST ELISABET Sahtouris' research offers us a perspective on why humans are presently so aggressive and competitive: it is not simply because it is in our nature; it is because we are young. Elisabet set out to study the origins of life and discovered an illuminating pattern. Here's what she found:

• Four billion years ago, all of life on this planet began as *single cells*. These single cells started out fiercely competitive, battling for nutrients, for the space to live and to grow. But over time, these combative cells began communicating and soon entered into a state of cooperation. Out of that cooperation, single cells created a new life form called *nucleated cells*. Nucleated cells then went through the same process: they began life competitive, suffered the pains of that competition, began "talking" to each other, and then entered into a state of cooperation. Out of that cooperation nucleated cells created another life form, *multicelled creatures,* from which the human species arose. Here's where things get interesting: Since the human species is only 175,000 years old, just a fraction of the four-billion-year total of life on this planet, Sahtouris theorizes that human beings are still in their feisty and competitive stage, and like our single-celled ancestors, we are now moving from a state of competition into a state of cooperation by talking to each other via such innovations as the Internet. And if we succeed, like the natural world before us, we, too, will begin to thrive and enter into a long-term state of creativity, harmony, and balance.

✳

HERE ARE JUST a few examples, a short and by no means exhaustive list, of recent scientific discoveries indicative of a species hardwired for connection:

- In 1976, a study published in the *Journal of Developmental Psychology* showed that 34-hour-old babies cry simply at the sound of other babies crying, demonstrating early *empathetic stress* at the distress of another.

- Numerous post–World War II studies confirm that the need for love and connection is so primal that orphaned babies who are not cuddled, who are deprived of affection, become sickly, weak, and even die.

- Through a serendipitous series of discoveries while studying macaque monkeys, scientists now know that all human beings are hardwired with *mirror neurons,* a biological trait that allows one to feel the pain of another. Thus, when an individual observes another taking a blow—a hit to the head or a kick to the crotch—the observer will feel the pain himself! These neurons are believed to be the biological basis for empathy.

- A new field of science called neurocardiology, which studies the human heart, has discovered that our hearts emit a measurable electromagnetic signal that extends up to 10 to 15 feet from the body. Furthermore, the wavelengths of this heart signal vary according to the emotional state of an individual: if a person is appreciative and happy, one signal is emitted; discontent and sad, a different signal is sent. Incredibly, these electromagnetic signals automatically link up with and affect others in our proximity. Thus, when a man or woman enters a room upset, joyful, happy, or sad, other individuals nearby register his or her emotional state and are instantly affected.

- After decades of studying the human body, doctors now know that aggressive, angry, and frustrated states break down human physiology. Living in these "negative" states contributes to the onset of numerous diseases, including heart attacks, headaches, digestive disorders, diabetes, compromised immune functions, and shortened life spans. The opposite is true for those who live in more "positive" states of love, gratitude, joy, and appreciation. These individuals experience more robust health outcomes and longer life spans.

- Science has also proven that negative emotional states such as anger and frustration impair cognitive functions. Hence the saying, *"A mad athlete is a bad athlete."* On the other hand, positive emotional states such as joy and gratitude lead to optimal cognitive function and enhanced athletic, artistic, and even job-related performance. This state of harmony and optimal productivity is known as *flow;* the athlete in the zone, the painter at one with the canvas.

- The Human Genome Project used DNA encoding to trace the origins of the human race. What they found is nothing short of remarkable: *all human beings come from two common ancestors in sub-Saharan Africa.* In other words, the entire human race shares the same ancestral parents, making us in fact, one big family. Saints and sages have told us this for millennia, that we are all brothers and sisters, and now science has proven exactly that!

Dialogue Eleven:

FEAR: I don't know where to start, there is so much to dispute here.
TRUTH: Start with your most basic objection; that you find all of this too hard to believe.

FEAR: And you believe all of this too easily! You believe without proper evidence.
TRUTH: And what is proper evidence?

FEAR: Evidence is evidence. Science is evidence.

TRUTH: The studies mentioned *are* science. But I do not limit my consideration of "evidence" to what you call science. I consider human experience over the millennia evidence. I consider the teachings of the poets and prophets across the centuries evidence, as well.

FEAR: The poets and prophets? What do they have to say about how life works, about science?

TRUTH: Apparently, a great deal. Is it not compelling that what these saints and sages have intuited over thousands of years—that we are all brothers and sisters—science is now confirming?

FEAR: So you think the saints and sages of yesterday were ahead of today's scientists? Just because they spouted some philosophical trope about our brotherhood? The mystics are dreamers. They speak in generalities. Nothing more.

TRUTH: Rilke's poetry is quite specific: *"There's a power in me to grasp and give shape to my world. I know that nothing has ever been real without my beholding it. All becoming has needed me . . ."* Consider Hafiz: *"Without me all shape would collapse."* These visions are the basis of quantum mechanics.

FEAR: Your claim is conjecture, completely subjective. It is not science. Science is measurable, quantifiable.

TRUTH: So you believe something has to be measurable to be real?

FEAR: That's the basis of science, yes.

TRUTH: Can science measure how much a mother loves her son? Does this make the experience any less real? Can science quantify the feeling in your heart when you look at the night sky painted with electric stars?

FEAR: These experiences may be real, but they cannot be counted as evidence.

TRUTH: And why not?

FEAR: Because a feeling is not scientific!

TRUTH: Are you aware of your prejudice? Do you say something isn't religious, so therefore you don't believe it? Do you say something isn't spiritual, so it's not credible? But you do say something has to be *scientific* before you hold it as true.

FEAR: Of course I do! Science is provable, it's demonstrable!

TRUTH: But science is imperfect and has often been wrong. Even the discoveries mentioned herein will one day be expanded upon, further credited or discredited. Why discount profound human experiences such as love, intuition, or the power of prayer because they do not fit neatly along the edges of your yardstick?

FEAR: I am not like you. I don't go off believing the first piece of fringe science to fall in my lap. I need more proof before I become a believer.

TRUTH: More proof of what, that mankind is hardwired for good?

FEAR: For starters, yes. I believe what I see. And what I see is a violent and aggressive species.

TRUTH: What you see, you have been trained to see. Look at life, all of life, and you will see something quite different. You will see love, and love all around. What is the basis of gravity, after all, but attraction? And what is love at its roots, but attraction?

FEAR: What I see is men killing each other: wars, rape, massacres at schools.

TRUTH: And you are so focused on the massacre, the single act of one lone gunman, that you miss the outpouring of love the world over, the countless tears of connection, the millions of prayers offered for healing, the incalculable acts of compassion in response to the shadow.

FEAR: Oh, please. Love shows up for a week and then man returns to what he is, violent and aggressive in his nature.

TRUTH: And if this is true, that mankind is simply violent and aggressive, why do these negative states break down his physiology? When he lives in these states, why do they bring about early onset diseases, from diabetes to ulcers to immune disorders? Why do pathways to the brain restrict when humans are angry and aggressive? If we were hardwired for this type of aggression, why would man not flourish in these states? And conversely, why do positive states renew physiology? Why do compassionate states— states of love, peace, and appreciation—boost immune function and reduce the onset of stress-related disease? Why does laughter heal, and why do positive emotions such as joy and gratitude hasten recovery and improve circulation and performance? You ask for science; this is science. Indisputable science.

FEAR: But it is also indisputable that aggression and competition drive the human species. Just look at the economy. The economy is full of competition.
TRUTH: And is it working? The economy?

FEAR: Well, not exactly. Not at the moment. But the economy will be fixed soon enough.
TRUTH: If the economy is acting outside of the way life works, it will not be fixed. It will never be fixed.

FEAR: That's ridiculous. The economy has worked well in the past, and it will work well again soon.
TRUTH: The economy has worked well for some. But for many it does not work. Do you know why?

FEAR: It's complicated.
TRUTH: It's actually quite simple. In fact, you have given us a good place to start. Let's consider our economy and how it works. Or perhaps, why it doesn't work.

ECONO-ME

✳

We have a greed with which we have agreed.

—JERRY HANNAN

OF ALL THE THINGS I TALK ABOUT and the philosophies I espouse, none gets treated with more disagreement, more diametric opposition, even disdain, than my views on our economy. I've been called a socialist more times than I can count. I'm not a socialist, I assure you, and don't even fully know what the term means; like *Christian,* it is a catchall that holds such widely divergent figures from the founder of the KKK to Kirk Cameron. But name-calling is fear's first line of defense, and with the name comes the sealed box that reduces human complexity to a checklist of prejudice and convenience. As long as we can find the right incendiary label, be it Republican, Democrat, Christian, Jew, Socialist, Communist, Gay, Straight, Left-wing, or Right-wing we stop learning in its tracks. Definition is the death of discovery, and if this dialogue is to have any merit, any chance of opening us up to new ideas and possibilities, let us keep our boxes at bay. For if you, the reader, can remain open, perhaps you will find yourself awakened to principles that, when applied to my own economic life, shook me to the fiscal and philosophical core.

Please understand—I am not an economist and don't pretend to be one. But that's a good thing, since I am also not subservient to the current system and its tenets. Expertise can be as much of a weight as a light, if we find ourselves stubbornly defending and not truly seeing. As Upton Sinclair noted, *"It is difficult to get a man to understand something, when his salary depends on his not understanding it."* My hope is that you can, even in your imagination, let go of your salary and be free to examine our system, the values it holds dear, and its grossly apparent absurdities.

Dialogue Twelve:

FEAR: At least you are off to an honest start. You admit to knowing nothing about the subject.
TRUTH: This is what I know: all biological systems are subject to the same laws, and when they are in violation of those laws, those systems do not survive.

FEAR: Again, your ignorance is on display. An economy is not a biological system.
TRUTH: It is a living system, and it is therefore subject to the laws of how things work.

FEAR: You are telling me the same laws that apply to a rain forest or an ant colony apply to an economy?
TRUTH: Or an oak tree, or a coral reef, or a nucleated cell.

FEAR: But human beings are different. We are more complex, and the systems we create cannot be so easily dissected.
TRUTH: Whether or not humans complicate a matter is not the

issue. The rules by which any living system operates are simple and consistent.

FEAR: The same rules that apply to a spreadsheet apply to a sunrise?
TRUTH: If the subject of that spreadsheet is a system that wishes to live and to thrive, yes. Thoreau said, *"The sun is but a morning star."* I would add, a morning star that daily demonstrates an economy that works.

FEAR: And by works, you mean . . . ?
TRUTH: It is an economy that supports life, that helps life thrive.

FEAR: And what is that economy?
TRUTH: The sun freely receives and freely gives in return.

FEAR: This is an economy? No wonder you are called a socialist!
TRUTH: Your labels will not keep the laws of life at bay. And the laws of life will exact an effect, whether you are in agreement with them or not.

FEAR: Fine, tell me about these laws.
TRUTH: First, we must examine laws that claim to be laws. Man-made laws. Laws that are not laws.

LAWS THAT ARE NOT LAWS

*

It's hard to overcome adversity;
it's even harder to overcome prosperity.

—ZEN PROVERB

THERE IS A PLAIN TRUTH about the economic laws and system that now control our collective fate. It is a truth so simple, so obvious, that it goes by without regard. That truth is this: *it's all made up.* Lest you think I'm exaggerating or kidding, I assure you I am not. Our economy is something we invented. The stock exchange, the S&P 500, the commodities index, interest rates, inflation, and devaluation are all inventions in a game we play called *economy.* Like football or foosball, we proclaim winners and losers, but unlike the world of sports, we hold economic losses as real, for some a matter of life and death—survival in the most primitive sense. We only have to turn on the news to see far too many losing at this game—a game no one seems to know how to fix, or why or where it's broken. Here's the good news: it hasn't always been this way, it doesn't have to be this way, and there are numerous examples of civilizations that have done things differently. The Tarahumara Indians developed a simple economy trading beer and favors; the San Bushmen of the Kalahari Desert share wealth evenly and freely; the Iroquois would make no major decision without first considering its effects on seven generations in the future. Alternative economies abound that have proven sustainable, if not wiser, over tens of thousands of years, and thus, is it not prudent to explore with an open mind, why, in comparison to people we call primitive, our approach to the economy may be failing?

Let's begin here in Southern California, where the news just proclaimed a startling statistic: since the economic collapse in 2008, California has lost more than 80 billion dollars in real estate value. This shocking statistic is not just due to the many homes hit with foreclosures. According to the laws of economics (which are not laws, as we'll soon see), when a home goes down in value, so do all of the other homes around it. So when your neighbor defaults, your home is devalued as well. There's more startling news: since 2008, the world's economy has lost— are you sitting down?—34.4 trillion dollars. Gulp. That's 34 trillion, with a "t." If you weren't startled before, then start your startled engines!

But here's what's really startling about all of this: We buy into this game of smoke and mirrors; we let it control us, our minds, our moods, our present, our future, our lives. And it is actually a game of smoke and mirrors. If we pull the curtain back and look, really look, there's nothing there; like *The Wizard of Oz,* there is no substance behind the voice of dread and doom, just the illusory cries of analysts, bankers and brokers, and a media caught up in the madness, pulling our strings, exacerbating our collective fears.

It's hard to comprehend this point because we're so blinded by the delusion that all of this is real. But stretch your mind for a moment, and consider that nothing real has been lost since 2008. Let that sink in . . . *Nothing real has been lost in the current economic crisis.* When Hurricane Katrina hit New Orleans in

2005, the losses there were tangible—houses were destroyed, infrastructure was damaged, lives were lost. The same can be said of Hurricane Sandy—real damage; real loss. Or when the 2011 tsunami hit Japan—more homes, more infrastructure, more lives gone. But what was lost in our economic tsunami? No one's home was destroyed; there were no floods; no buildings were damaged. Everything is still standing. All infrastructure is still intact. So what changed? Numbers on a piece of paper. The scoreboard changed. *Perception changed.*

"But what about all of those people who lost their life savings when the market crashed, or lost their homes? That seems pretty darn real, doesn't it?" It has become real, certainly, and there are people who are hurting. But trace the root of that suffering, and what you find is quite disturbing. You find willful choices, man set against his fellow man, accepted societal selfishness based on the delusion of our separation; our collective agreement to abide by the controlling idea of the economic game—that all is opportunity for profit; everything, the economy tells us, is for sale.

What we have lost is not the reality of sticks and stones, blood and sinew, meat and marrow, but *vision*, the reality of our connection and inherent brotherhood. People kicked families out of homes when they didn't have to. Fear overtook the market, causing it to plummet, but we didn't have to give in to that fear. Our markets are a reflection of the people who create and sustain them. Our markets will stabilize when we stabilize. Two words and two words alone could have solved the foreclosure crisis: *You're good.* But we chose not to work things out with each other; we chose profits over people. Look beneath the story we're being told and a truth becomes evident:

we don't ultimately have a crisis of credit, we have a crisis of compassion. Some will undoubtedly call this assertion naïve, but since when is making the well-being of another naïve? *Our economy plummeted not because any value was lost, but because we've lost our values.*

Nowhere is this crisis more apparent than in our blind belief in economic laws that are not laws; for example, the law of supply and demand. We teach this law to young and old alike, declaring it immutable, like gravity or a gale force wind. But it's not a law. Sitting beside me as I write this is a glass of water. The law of supply and demand states that if this is the last glass of water in all of Southern California, its price increases. But that's not a law, that's a choice. Yes, its *value* increases, but I can just as easily share this water freely as charge a thousand dollars a sip. No mandatory law goes into effect with scarcity. An apple is still an apple, not more or less so, even if it's the last of its kind. It takes a person with a very specific agenda to raise the price of that apple, making it a hardship for some to acquire.

And with a belief in a law that is not a law come more delusions. Inflation, for example, is not some natural force, like thermodynamics or entropy; it's our collective fear made manifest. Your economic textbooks will tell you otherwise—that inflation is the result of governments printing excess currency, which devalues the worth of a dollar, or when the supply of material goods goes down, prices naturally rise. But prices don't naturally rise—people choose to raise those prices. What your textbook won't tell you is that these inflationary figures and trends are, again, based on choices. It's a chain reaction really, and the first link in that chain is fear: if the price of a good or service is going up, I've got to charge an extra nickel for the bread I sell; if the consumer is paying an extra nickel for his bread, then he's got to charge a dime more for his accounting services; and so on and so forth. Trace the rising cost of a good or service back to its roots and you will find that price increases routinely begin as willful choices, and willful choices are not laws.

Dialogue Thirteen:

FEAR: With regard to the economy, you say, unfairly, that it is all made up. That it's been invented. But everything is made up! The way we educate, organize society, form governments, even your name is made up!

TRUTH: And so these things can be remade, can they not?

FEAR: But the question shouldn't be, *Is the economy made up?* but *Is the economy working?*

TRUTH: And is it working? In this country alone, nearly one in four children goes to bed hungry each night. Worldwide, 1 percent of the population owns 40 percent of the wealth and one billion people live on less than one dollar a day. There's more, if you care to listen—from the European collapse to the global credit crisis.

FEAR: You can't just look at the economy in the short term, when we're in a downturn. You have to look at it over a long period of time.

TRUTH: These gaps, these inequities, are nothing new. Like all poison, it has simply seeped over time. And what is this poison? It is the values, the mind-set, that animate our current system.

FEAR: What good will this do, all this talk of values? It is more empty idealism.

TRUTH: The values that undergird a system will tell you precisely what will spring forth from that system. The problems in the present-day economy are not accidental. They are direct outgrowths of a value system, a mind-set that reflects back its own mirror image.

FEAR: This sounds like another indictment of the rich. More finger pointing and beating the drum of class warfare.

TRUTH: The finger points to all who embrace the mind-set of the current economy, rich and poor alike, the middle class and the upwardly mobile.

FEAR: And this mind-set you consider so egregious is what exactly?

TRUTH: The commoditization of everything, the admiration and elevation of those who acquire and accumulate the most.

FEAR: But the rich acquire the most, the rich accumulate the most. Are you not indicting them for doing so?

TRUTH: No more than the poor who envy them, thus doing their share to continue the pervasiveness of the poison and keep things as they are.

FEAR: Can we not talk more practically? You say there are numerous examples of alternative economies, economies that have proven wiser and more sustainable. Give me one example of such an economy and I will riddle your logic with holes.
TRUTH: Humankind's oldest living ancestor, the San Bushmen of the Kalahari Desert.

FEAR: The San Bushmen? Ha! They are primitive! They still live in huts and forage for food!
TRUTH: It is irrelevant whether they live in huts or houses. What is relevant are the principles on which they have sustained themselves for more than 50,000 years.

FEAR: But we have technology, science, medical advances. We do not wish to live as they live!
TRUTH: To remain alive is what we do wish, and they have managed to do so longer than any other society.

FEAR: And you say it is because of principles?
TRUTH: The principles on which they base their lives, and thus their economy.

FEAR: So what are these principles? What has sustained the Bushmen for 50,000 years?
TRUTH: The principles are best illustrated by the story of the anthropologists who first studied the Bushmen. In order to gain favor with the tribe, the initial research team regularly shared their food, offering the natives various treats. But not only was

no apparent favor gained, the Bushmen never said so much as a thank-you.

FEAR: That's what I'm saying! Any tribe not human enough to show gratitude isn't worthy of our consideration!

TRUTH: There is more to the story. The more time the researchers spent with the Bushmen, the more a principle began to reveal itself—*Food sharing is the accepted norm among the Bushmen.* In fact, the Bushmen will share the last of their food even with a stranger, as they believe that one day that stranger may help feed them. This practice is so commonplace that no thank-you is considered necessary.

FEAR: What do you mean, no thank-you is necessary? All civilized people show some kind of appreciation when food is shared.

TRUTH: And this is the point. Food sharing in today's society is not the norm, and when practiced, gratitude is expected. For the Bushmen, it is a way of life.

FEAR: I don't see how showing gratitude is a bad thing!

TRUTH: It is not a bad thing; it is simply not needed.

FEAR: Among the civilized, gratitude is always welcome and always needed!

TRUTH: Is it? Do you thank the driver in front of you for stopping at a red light?

FEAR: What do you mean?

TRUTH: Do you get out of your car, run up to the car in front of you, tap on the window, and yell, *"Thank you!"*

FEAR: No, of course not!

TRUTH: Why don't you?

FEAR: They'd think you were crazy!

TRUTH: And why would they think this?

FEAR: The person in front of you is just obeying the law. It's no big deal. It's expected.

TRUTH: As is food sharing among the Bushmen. It's no big deal; it's expected. Just like stopping at a traffic light, no thank-you is needed.

FEAR: Okay, they share food. Is that really such a big thing? Does it make their society so different from ours?

TRUTH: Radically different. Do you understand what an economy reflects in a society?

FEAR: The way people do business, I suppose.

TRUTH: The way people do business *is* the economy. But what does this reflect?

FEAR: I don't know. What they care about?

TRUTH: An economy reflects the values a society holds dear, what it lives for, what principles it stands upon. The Bushmen value the well-being of the entire community, and thus, their economy makes goods and services equally available to all. Inflation does not exist among the San Bushmen; it never has, and if they hold fast to their traditions, it never will. Nor does poverty. In fact, you will never find a Bushman starving while others are well fed. That's right, there has never been a poor person among the Bushmen, and there never will be. Not as long as the Bushmen adhere to the principles that sustain their economy.

FEAR: But they have no money, none of the finer things in life. No technology. The Bushmen are *all* poor!
TRUTH: The Bushmen live off the land. That is not poverty. Not as poverty exists in today's society.

FEAR: And how do you define poverty as it exists in today's society?
TRUTH: When one person cannot meet his or her basic needs for food, medicine, and shelter, while others have more than they need. In today's society, these people often exist within blocks of each other, the well-to-do behind gates, the poor suffering in ghettos and slumlike conditions. This kind of poverty is unheard of in tribal cultures. In fact, poverty and slavery did not even exist until the advent of agriculture, when mankind first embraced the mentality that allowed these phenomena to rise up in the first place.

FEAR: This is hard to believe. Are you saying no one has ever starved among the Bushmen or other tribes?
TRUTH: No, I am not saying that. I am saying no one is considered poor. If wild game is scarce and foraging proves fruitless, *all* the Bushmen may go hungry, never just one. The Bushmen live and

die, suffer and thrive, together, as one tribe. The way the tribe handles food, medicine, and shelter—in other words, the way they practice economy—tells you quite clearly what the Bushmen value, what they care about. And what they care about is each other.

FEAR: You know what this sounds like? Another form of socialism. Socialism in bare feet and a loincloth.

TRUTH: The Bushmen are not socialists. No system or individual forces them to behave this way. They behave this way by choice, because it has proven beneficial in ensuring their tribe not only survives but thrives. And for 50,000 years, it has done just that.

FEAR: I still say the Bushmen are not a realistic comparison. Their system is too simplistic. Even you have said they do not have inflation. They do not have a housing crisis.

TRUTH: The question is, *why* don't they have inflation? *Why* don't they have a housing crisis?

FEAR: I know what you will say—because of their values, their mind-set!

TRUTH: Exactly. Our values have created our current crises. What we hold to be true internally plays itself out externally. Fixing our economy is not a matter of a stimulus package here or a financial jolt there. It is our values, our mind-set, that must be examined and called into question.

FEAR: And this is true, say, of the housing collapse?

TRUTH: A perfect illustration. Thousands of people have been kicked out of their homes, correct?

FEAR: And for good reason. They could not pay what they owed!

TRUTH: You are aware that many of these houses are still sitting empty?

FEAR: What does that matter?

TRUTH: How do you think a Bushmen would view this?

FEAR: It's not relevant how a Bushman would view this! They don't even have houses!

TRUTH: Again, whether they have huts or houses is not the issue. They take care of each other. This is what matters. They value community above all. So how would they view this?

FEAR: As unacceptable, I suppose.

TRUTH: As insane. The houses are just sitting there. Why not let people live in them?

FEAR: Because these people would not learn their lesson!

TRUTH: And you believe there is only one way to learn a lesson? You do not believe in the power of love and generosity to instruct as well as discipline?

FEAR: Holding people accountable is a form of love. It's tough love!

TRUTH: Must tough love go so far? Must tough love turn a child out into the streets?

FEAR: These people overreached through their own greed. They made a mistake, and they must pay for that mistake. Who are you to ask that they be forgiven?

TRUTH: Your spiritual disciplines do not ask, they command. As Jesus taught, *"When your brother asks for your shirt, give him your coat, as well . . ." "How many times must I forgive? Seven times? I say unto you, not seven times, but seventy times seven."* How do you reconcile such teachings?

FEAR: They are platitudes and nothing more.

TRUTH: Then they should be discarded along with the saints and sages who espoused them. What good are such teachings if they do not work in the real world?

FEAR: So what are you saying, if we do not adopt the Bushmen's principles . . . ?

TRUTH: We will go the path of all living systems that choose to operate outside of how things work.

FEAR: Poverty and inflation will render us extinct?

TRUTH: The principles and values that create poverty and inflation will render us extinct.

GROWTH IS GOOD

✳

When I hear the stock market has fallen, I say,
"Long live gravity!"

—WENDELL BERRY

I RECENTLY RECEIVED AN E-MAIL from a real-estate broker that boasts, *"Some good news! Real-estate prices rose for the third consecutive month!"* This left me thinking, who exactly is this good news for? Perhaps the broker or the property holder seeing dollar signs in place of real-estate signs. But what about the low-income prospective buyer, the housekeeper or the janitor, the waiter or waitress, the teacher or maintenance man, who can barely afford to feed their families, now forced to enter a housing market whose inflation we so blindly declare as *"good news!"*? Why is it that we so universally accept that rising real-estate prices, or commodity prices, or stock market prices, ought to be celebrated like a baby's birth or a teen boy's bar mitzvah? What is it we are so readily cheering? The answer is *growth,* the value we hold above all others, the driver of the engine we call economy. "Gross domestic product *grew* by 3 percent!" "The housing market *grew* for the third straight month!" "Private sector jobs *grew* faster than expected." "America's market share *grew* in relation to the European Union." Daily, the message is plainly laid out before us—growth is the barometer by which we measure our system's health and vitality.

"But," one might object, *"doesn't our system also value hard work, persistence, conscience, and integrity?"* To a point, certainly, but when was the last time you heard a newscaster say, *"The Hard Work Index rose three quarters of a percent as American workers steadily increased their efforts"*? After all, GDP stands for gross domestic product, not gross domestic persistence! Or, have you ever heard a reporter declare, *"The Economic Integrity Indicator rose this month, as more workers told the truth in their business dealings"*? In fact, isn't the opposite often the case, with our system regularly rewarding not honesty, but dishonesty? Who, after all, gained the most from the recent economic crisis? Those venture capitalists, bankers, and default swappers who sold the public faulty loans based on half-truths, if not outright lies. Yes, we might applaud honesty and hard work in conversations around the water cooler, but they are not the benchmarks for economic success. Otherwise, wouldn't the ditch digger be on economic par with the CEO? No one worked harder than the caterers on *Evan Almighty.* They rose at 3 A.M. every morning to shop for us, cook for us, and feed us, but they were paid little in comparison to the stars, producers, and well, me. (The kitchen staff, I later found out, lived three and four to a room, as many could not afford a place to stay.) But cooks are not paid handsomely, nor are ditch diggers, or teachers, or policemen, or firefighters, because generally, they don't "grow" businesses. Rather, our economy rewards the growers because growth, right up there with greed, is good. But is it?

Declaring growth our god ignores a law that is actually a law: *in a closed system, nothing can grow forever.* And we do in fact, live in a closed system. There is only one earth, so much oil, so many trees, and a limited supply of air and water. Thus, we see signs of our chosen motivator, growth, eating away at finite resources at a pace never before seen in history. Here's a deeply disturbing statistic from Jeremy Rifkin's book, *The Empathic Civilization: The human species is less than 1 percent of the biomass on this planet, but we are currently using 24 percent of the world's energy generated by sunlight and photosynthesis.* As renowned researcher Jonas Salk points out, *if all the insects were to disappear from the earth, within 50 years, all life on earth would end; if all human beings disappeared from the earth, within 50 years, all forms of life would flourish.*

✳

So WHAT EXACTLY does this god of growth measure? It does not measure happiness, quality of life, satisfaction, fulfillment, meaning, or purpose. What it measures is singular and indicting; *it measures profits.* If profits are up, our economy is working. If profits are down, the ship is listing and needs to be righted. And by profits, of course, we mean money; money, which is supposed to make us happy and move our businesses forward. Money and money alone, we are told, drives ingenuity, creativity, risk, and progress. Without it, we teach our children, no one would have the incentive to build anything new. But doesn't money as the primary motivator ignore the deepest, most rewarding aspects of our lives—love, beauty, purpose, compassion, creativity, and serving a cause greater than ourselves? What motivated Jesus in his work as a teacher? Was it making money, or was it love? What motivated Mother Teresa to help the suffering souls dying alone on the streets of Calcutta? Was it a hefty retirement package, or was it compassion for those in need? What about the Peace Corps, the Red Cross, or Oxfam? Are they waiting to cash some dividend check to send their workers off to an early retirement, or are they serving their fellow man because it is blessed and beautiful to do so? What about St. Jude Children's Research Hospital, which treats kids with cancer for free? What about Paul Newman's Newman's Own, which gives 100 percent of its after-tax profits to charity? What about Invisible Children, a group that is freeing child soldiers and ending the longest-running war in Africa? All these organizations share a common motivation, *love,* and have found richer rewards in serving others than in the accumulation of material wealth.

But note, the cultural hum for growth and profits is so strong that we routinely describe our altruistic endeavors in negative terms—we call them *non*profits and *non*governmental agencies—as if it is not profitable to love your fellow man or to serve your community with your time and talent. In South America, the term *minga* means a social gathering for the common good—the people of a local village, for example, call a *minga* to fix a neighbor's roof, mend a road, or build a community well. Search as you might, there is no such term in the English language. *Barn raising* is as close as we come, and that now belongs to the Amish. Occasionally, Habitat for Humanity raises a roof, but again, this goes under the heading, *not-for-profit.* To call this powerful work *non*profit, is plainly put, *non*sense.

There is much more to this economic anarchy that we presently serve, including our blind omission of what economists term *externalities.* An externality is anything that the system refuses to account for in the production of a good or service. For example, we do not count the toxic runoff from chemical manufacturing that poisons our water supply; we don't count air pollution from carbon emissions in the making or running of the automobile; we don't count the lethal human health costs in the mining of coal. Somehow, economists don't consider these relevant in their narrowly drawn columns of profit and loss; but be assured, in the broader column of life, the chemically bleached soil that can no longer grow food and the family that loses a father to black lung register a loss that is painful and real.

How is it that a culture founded on the Judeo-Christian ethic—*"It is easier for a camel to pass through the eye of a needle than for a rich man to enter the kingdom of heaven"*—encourages its youth to not only become rich men, but puts them on magazine covers when they do? How is it that we embrace moral teachings which urge us *"do not store up treasures on earth,"* and then print lists praising those who do exactly that?

If there is only one thing to take away from this writing, let it be this: *our economic problems are not mechanical, they are moral.* If you start with a wrong question—*"How do we fix our economy?"*—you will likely end up with a wrong answer, derailed in detail and minutia. Is it not wise to ask a truer question? *"Who am I, and what values do I hold dear?"* If it is material wealth and personal gain, then the present mind-set will serve you well. If it is love, compassion, and equity, then a reinvention of how each of us approaches business is in order. For the solutions to moral questions can only be found in morality itself. We have looked long enough at market trends, twists, and turns. Is it not time we looked in a better place, a truer place . . . in the mirror?

Dialogue Fourteen:

FEAR: You say we live in a closed system and that there are limited resources. This contradicts certain beliefs, does it not? *The Secret.* The power of positive thinking. Do you believe in these?
TRUTH: I believe in truthful thinking.

FEAR: And what is wrong with positive thinking? You don't believe it works? You don't believe people can create whatever they want with their thoughts?
TRUTH: Why would someone want to do such a thing?

FEAR: Because they want something, more money, a house, a car.
TRUTH: But *why* do they want these things?

FEAR: What does it matter why? They want them because they want them, because their neighbor just got a new car!
TRUTH: In that case, no, I don't think the power of positive thinking works. If a person wants to attract something and that want comes from ego, what they ultimately will attract is difficulty.

FEAR: Why? They wanted a car, they got a car. What's the problem?
TRUTH: The problem is, a prayer for anything other than to do the will of God is meanness and theft. And when you sow the seed of meanness, meanness is what returns to you.

FEAR: People can't pray for things?

TRUTH: They can and they do. The question is, *why* are they praying for a thing? *The Secret* illuminates a truth, the law of cause and effect. The law of cause and effect does not bring you things; it brings you the seeds you sow. If you want something for selfish reasons, you sow the seed of selfishness and will reap its rotten fruit. If you seek something with a pure intention, you will reap the rewards of that purity.

FEAR: And what is a pure intention?

TRUTH: To offer yourself, your talents, your all, in service. To be *"a hole in a flute the Christ's breath moves through."*

FEAR: I have never understood this sentiment from Hafiz. To be a hole in a flute? What does that mean?

TRUTH: The God breath blows through each of us. The more we are full of ego, worldly impediments, the desire for power, to make a name for oneself or to set oneself apart, the more obstructed is the note we play. People wish for things, but the wish is not important; what is important is the willingness. When people move from the wish to the willing, they become free.

FEAR: The wish to the willing? What is that?

TRUTH: Wishes often come out of ego, out of self-centered desire; "I *wish* I could land that job." "I *wish* I could get that girl." Instead of wishing for something, move to the willing; "I am *willing* to serve God with all I am, whether or not this job manifests." "I am *willing* to offer myself in love regardless of the outcome."

FEAR: You talk out of both sides of your mouth. You say people who wish for things can be selfish but your Emerson praises people for being self-reliant. Do you not see your hypocrisy?
TRUTH: There is no hypocrisy here. Selfishness and self-reliance are opposites. Selfishness sees only the individual and his wants; it ignores the greater truth of our oneness and connection. Self-reliance is in touch with God within. It cannot be selfish, as one's own truth is in service of the greater Truth that connects all things. What is a Transcendentalist, after all, but one who transcends the illusion of our separation?

FEAR: But none of this talk of limits is very appealing. You cannot get very far with people if you are a glass-half-empty guy.
TRUTH: Whether the glass is half empty or half full is not my concern. I seek to know how many ounces are in the glass. If I say the glass is half empty, I create unnecessary worry over how much water remains. If I say it is half full, I create a false sense of security that has the water downed too quickly. If I know the glass contains eight ounces of water, my perspective is clear and true.

FEAR: But your approach seems negative. Why do you hold such a firm belief in limits and not in possibility?
TRUTH: To believe in limits is not to ignore possibility but to embrace it. To ignore limits is simply to deny what is. All of life has limits. The seasons have limits. Spring comes, but its days are numbered. As are the days of winter. There is only so much time in the calendar year. The sun's arc does not go on interminably across the sky; daylight always gives way to darkness. A human life has limits. Even Jesus himself did not

escape physical death. All art has limits. Drama has limits. Music has limits. The painter paints within the confines of a canvas. A cellist chooses a note, a progression, eliminating all other notes, all other progressions. This limit gives music its melody. All music tends toward silence. Silence is a limit. When one chooses to write a book, one has set a limit. Choose film, and another limit arises. All stories move forward by limits. Characters run into obstacles, essentially limits. These limits propel them into action. It is a great lie to believe all limits are to be avoided. Limits give life context and meaning. St. Francis often carried a human skull to remind him that his physical form was finite. He embraced the ultimate limit, physical death, and thus was moved to embrace life.

FEAR: There is one other point you bring up that is irresponsible: your statement that our problems are not mechanical but moral. This is a gross oversimplification. The world's problems are much more complicated than you make them out to be. This is a naïve assumption.

TRUTH: Is it naïve when you see hunger, to feed people? When you find inequity, to share resources? When you discover pollution, to respect the earth? When you experience war, to stand for peace?

FEAR: It's not that simple and you know it! There are bad people in the world, greedy people, violent people.

TRUTH: My concern is not with greedy or violent people. My concern is with you and the power you ignore. The power to heal the greed and violence in your own heart.

FEAR: This is symbolic only. It will do nothing. One person healing one's own heart isn't going to change anything.
TRUTH: One person changing, changes everything around him. The domino theory is not a theory, but a reality. Knock over a domino and watch what happens. Other dominos fall. Not sometimes, every time.

FEAR: If this is true, why hasn't everyone changed? Why hasn't change swept the landscape?
TRUTH: Change has happened, and it continues to happen. But the question here is not *why haven't others changed?* The question posed here is, *have you changed?* Are you adding to the greed in the world, or are you promoting justice and equity—not just in thought but in deed—in all areas of your life? Are you adding to the violence around you, or are you working for peace in your own heart, spreading love in each and every encounter?

FEAR: How futile this all is! So what if one or two people change. What difference will this make?
TRUTH: This is what the leaders in Egypt, Syria, and Yemen undoubtedly believed. And without warning, the Arab Spring emerged. A new spring is emerging now that many see. It is the new mind-set; humanity's awakening to a new world. The question now is, *are you doing your part to bring this new world forth?*

ALRIGHTY THEN!

❊

There is enough in the world for everyone's need,
but not enough for everyone's greed.

—FRANK BUCHMAN

IN FEBRUARY OF 1994, a little film called *Ace Ventura: Pet Detective* came out of nowhere to become one of the year's biggest sleeper hits. Now "out of nowhere," of course, was not out of nowhere—Jim Carrey had long been doing standup comedy, and I had been writing and studying film for the better part of a decade. But *Ace* accomplished something our previous work had not, and that something is, it made money—lots of it. *Ace* cost $11 million to produce, but it grossed over $100 million worldwide, causing the studio to joyfully shout the film's famous catchphrase, *"Alrighty then!"* And since the official car of Hollywood is not the limousine but the Brinks truck, *Ace* instantly announced the arrival of Jim and me on the feature-film scene.

I don't have to tell anyone about Jim's meteoric rise, so I'll focus here on my own. It wasn't as meteoric, but it certainly was a rise. Using today's accepted economic jargon, the demand for my services went up, and so did my price. Here's a look at my ascent into what I would term the salary stratosphere: On *Ace,* I was paid director's minimum, or scale, which at the time was around $140,000. On my second picture, *The Nutty Professor* starring Eddie Murphy, I was paid $2.8 million, which included a $1 million box office performance bonus. Next came *Liar, Liar,* and with base salary and bonuses, my take was $5 million. *Patch Adams* followed, and I received roughly $10 million. My next picture, *Bruce Almighty,* upon its release became the highest-grossing original comedy of all time, and so I was paid the astronomical sum of around $30 million. Finally, on *Evan Almighty,* which did not perform well at the box office (it made $100 million domestically but cost $175 million), I received a total of $9 million.

Now with five out of six hits as a comedy director, and with two successes as a producer (*Accepted* and *I Now Pronounce You Chuck and Larry*), one would think that all would be well in the world, certainly my world, but that wasn't the case. On the positive side, my track record at the box office afforded me a level of artistic freedom rarely granted to writers, directors, and filmmakers. On the down side, there came a kind of pressure for each picture to outdo the next, as both my expectations and the studio's rose along with the grosses. In addition, my personal life became more chaotic and complicated; I spent money freely, purchasing larger and larger houses, which needed artwork, furniture, staffing, maintenance, cleaning, and care. But the most surprising effect, and one I didn't anticipate, was how I felt about my disproportionate take: that it was neither good nor right. This wasn't good old-fashioned Catholic guilt, but a deep-seated knowing that somehow my life had spun out of balance and my excessive salary demands might be connected to and even a cause of the lack and inequity around me.

After *Liar, Liar* further fattened my wallet, I remember dining with a friend and sharing my strange urge to walk away from this windfall. I couldn't articulate exactly why, only that I didn't want to have so much, while others had so little. My friend, who was also a professional counselor, no doubt quelled the urge to scream *"Then give me some of it!"* and after listening patiently, respectfully objected to my white-collar woes. His argument was simple: the money was a blessing, and I could give more and more of it away.

I bit on this bait line of logic swallowing full hook and sinker and continued my swim with the sharks. But the seeds of intuition planted in my soul could not be kept from sprouting, and that fateful book, *Ishmael*, was just the dose of sunlight needed. But this was just the start of my awakening, as an even bigger revelation concerning *the workings of economy in the natural world* would shock me still further. As I would soon discover, *nature's economy is in diametric opposition to our own,* its efficiency and sustainability apparent in an oak tree or an elk herd. In the end, it is an economy whose wisdom and example may be the key to the survival of the human species. So how does it work, and what exactly is the root of its longevity and effectiveness?

Dialogue Fifteen:

FEAR: You say your disproportionate take did not feel right. But your price went up because you were making the studio money. What's wrong with that? What's wrong with taking all you can?

TRUTH: Taking all you can is not a behavior reflected in nature or living systems. Not living systems that seek to thrive in the long run.

FEAR: But mankind does not have to live like nature. Man can make his own laws.

TRUTH: And as long as those laws are outside of nature and the way things work, he will be subject to the consequences of those invented laws.

FEAR: And what consequences were you subject to? None, other than guilt!

TRUTH: Money is energy. And with the arrival of disproportionate amount of energy comes responsibility in kind. Energy needs to move. It wants to flow out. It wants to flow back.

FEAR: So you let it flow out. You bought things.

TRUTH: Which also came with energy.

FEAR: Meaning what? The things you bought you had to take care of? You had a staff!

TRUTH: And the staff that was taking care of things also had to be taken care of. The fact is, the life I had fallen into was not my own.

FEAR: And what life did you want? The life of a pauper, of a hermit?

TRUTH: I wanted a life of service, of integrity. Integrity means wholeness. A person who demonstrates integrity lives a unified life.

FEAR: What do you mean, a unified life?

TRUTH: If you look in any drawer of a man's life, you will know who he is. When I looked in the drawer of my fiscal life, I did not like what I saw there.

FEAR: You saw success. And you have a fear of success!
TRUTH: What I saw was hypocrisy.

FEAR: But it is not money, it is the love of money that is the root of all evil.
TRUTH: And what was I loving by asking for so much? Certainly not the natural world from which this material wealth came. Certainly not my fellow man.

FEAR: You are not responsible for your fellow man.
TRUTH: I am responsible *to* him. And when an individual takes so much and sets himself apart, others are affected. Trace the money back; what is found there is quite disturbing. Tremendous wealth is routinely built on the backs of others; on the labor of others that is undervalued, underappreciated, and underrewarded—the janitor who sweeps the floor of the stage upon which we act out our play; the caterer who serves food that gives us the strength to complete our work; the security guard who watches our equipment nightly as we sleep.

FEAR: But you are the director! According to the laws of economics, you are the most valuable!
TRUTH: The laws of economics are the inventions of man. There is a higher law at work that is immutable and true. Emerson spoke about it, Jesus spoke about it, and Gandhi spoke about it—it is the law of love. And from that law, we must infer that a basic level of subsistence and dignity for all is natural and just. My greed—there's no other word for it, really—made it harder for the

common laborer to reach that level of dignity, for nature itself to remain in balance.

FEAR: But what do you have to do with this? It's just the system. And that system is already in place.

TRUTH: And by saying yes to the system, I was saying yes to the injustice the system supports. Slavery was a system. Women were once property. This was also a system. Individuals saw the injustice of these systems and refused to obey them. The same must be true of our economy—this insatiable need to accumulate more and have it all. Is it not enough to know that you have served others with all that you are? Is this not a truer wealth than the accumulation of money, power, and things?

FEAR: I don't understand your complaint. The money you made did not come from the janitor. It came from the audience members who saw your movies.

TRUTH: It is not a question of where the money came from. It is a question of taking more than I needed.

FEAR: And you don't think that's fair? Well, life isn't fair!

TRUTH: It's currently not fair because we do not behave fairly. When our hearts beat with love and equity, the world will reflect that love and equity. We cannot expect a world at peace until we ourselves have become peace.

FEAR: You expect too much.

TRUTH: Is it not society that expects too much? To keep up with the Joneses? To set yourself apart? As Hafiz implores us, *"Why go to* *sleep tonight exhausted from the folly of ignorance?"* And what is this ignorance? That you are incomplete. That you always need more. Let it go, and rest in the knowledge that brings freedom.

FEAR: And what is this knowledge?
TRUTH: The knowledge that *you already are.*

FEAR: I already am?
TRUTH: Now remove the question mark.

THE LION AND THE GAZELLE

✳

Never does nature say one thing and wisdom another.

—JUVENAL, SATIRES

*When we have seen Reality there is not a grain
of dust which has not a sublime meaning.*

—J. J. VAN DER LEEUW

LIFE, OR NATURE, began on this planet some four billion years ago. In those four billion years, a law has become evident that is immutable and true; in fact, all biological systems that thrive in the long run obey this law; all systems that violate this law will eventually die off. Here's the law: *nothing in nature takes more than it needs.* That bears repeating: *nothing in nature takes more than it needs.* Think about it. A redwood tree doesn't take all of the soil's nutrients; it just takes what it needs to grow. A lion doesn't kill every gazelle, it just kills one. In fact, when the lion has fed, gazelles will go on grazing right in the lion's midst. Why? Certainly, the lion could pounce again, but it doesn't. Somehow, the lion naturally obeys this life-giving law of limits, a law that keeps nature in balance and keeps the delicate cycle upon which all of life depends intact.

Contrary to what we have been taught, *cooperation,* not competition, is the ruling order of nature. An ocean, a rain forest, even the human body, are all cooperatives. A coral reef, for example, provides food in the form of plant life for pilot fish; pilot fish, in turn, excrete waste onto coral reefs, providing food for more plant life. An oak tree receives sustenance from the soil, and in turn gives back leaves, twigs, and fallen branches that decompose and sustain the soil. All of nature exists in a grand web of connection, and any broken links in that web can have disastrous consequences.

On the rare occasion that nature does give rise to a rogue species that violates the law of limits, she soon acts as judge and jury, exacting a consistent and harsh penalty: death. The kudzu vine, for example, is a particularly parasitic specimen that overtakes everything in its path. But watch a kudzu vine over a long span of time. It may take a thousand years, or a million years, but a kudzu vine's unchecked growth would inevitably lead to its own demise. How? By eliminating biodiversity, an essential condition for life—the first freeze could kill it off. And so, by choking out all other plant life, the kudzu vine would eventually choke itself out. The same fate would apply to the rabbits of Australia, or any animal, vegetable, or mineral that does not honor the law of limits.

Tragically, mankind, with our unchecked appetite for more, violates this law every day. We are encouraged and even rewarded for taking as much as we can, a philosophy that has had catastrophic consequences: we have overfished the oceans, devastated the rain forests, and are now pushing countless animal species to the brink of extinction. Ironically, we understand well just how deadly an organism can be that grows without limits. In fact, we have a term for cells in the body that take more than their share—we call those cells *cancer*. And if we persist in this unchecked behavior, we will inevitably succumb to the same fate of all cancerous cells: *we will die off.*

When I applied the law of limits to my own economic life, I saw that I, too, was behaving as a kind of cancerous cell. I was not just taking what I needed; I was taking all I could get. My economic philosophy was rotten at its roots. I immediately began to rethink how I could approach my business life in a way that reflected the wisdom and sustainability of nature. And a new question began to form. Instead of asking, *"How much can I get?"* I began to ask, *"How much do I need?"* And not just how much do I need to survive, but how much do I need to thrive. For ultimately, nature does not preach a gospel of austerity, but of plentitude. And so, for the next several years, I sought the answer to a question that would change the course of my life: *"How much do I need to lead a life that is meaningful, purposeful, and joyful?"*

Dialogue Sixteen:

FEAR: So you are saying basically anyone who is rich is acting outside of nature's laws by taking more than they need?
TRUTH: I am not saying that at all. I am saying *I* took more than *I* needed.

FEAR: But admit it. You are judging others. You moved from a mansion to a mobile home, so you want others to do the same. You simplified your life, so you want others to seek simplicity.
TRUTH: What I want for others is what is true for them. What rests in their hearts. If it is true for you to reside in a mansion, then

do so. If it is true that a simpler life calls to you, then heed that call. If we value the wisdom of nature the question we must all ask is, *"How much is enough?"*

FEAR: Ah, so the truth comes out. You want people to sacrifice. You want them to have less.

TRUTH: I want them to have more. More authenticity. More connection. More life. The message has been the same for two thousand years: *"I have come so you could have life and have it more abundantly."*

FEAR: The carpenter's words are hypocritical. Jesus spoke of abundance, but he himself was poor. He knew nothing of abundance, except in suffering.

TRUTH: Suffering was a part of his abundance, yes. As was love, grace, and mercy.

FEAR: Why don't you say what you really think: when you share your wealth with others you become truly wealthy.

TRUTH: It is not what I think. It is what I experience every day.

FEAR: Ah, yes. Just what the world needs, another socialist who wishes to redistribute wealth.

TRUTH: I do not wish to redistribute wealth; I wish to redefine it. When people understand that true wealth is found not in the accumulation of things, but in the advancement of love, wealth will redistribute itself.

FEAR: Who can relate to you—or any of the rich? Most people do not even have money to share.
TRUTH: Everyone has something to share; their time, their talent, a kind word.

FEAR: Money matters more. Just ask those without it.
TRUTH: So the poet's admonition is wrong? *"You give but little when you give of your possessions. It is when you give of yourself that you truly give."*

FEAR: Ugh, Gibran. Your distant cousin. He has poisoned you.
TRUTH: He has awakened me. Whatever we do for another, we do for ourselves. All things are bound together. All things connect.

FEAR: Everything is one; is that where this is going?
TRUTH: It is not a matter of going, it is already there.

TWENTY-FOUR DOLLARS

✳

You have forgotten the One
who doesn't care about ownership,
who doesn't try to turn a profit
from every human exchange.

—RUMI

IN 1997, I DIRECTED and produced *Patch Adams,* a film about a real-life medical doctor who refused to commoditize his patients' ailments. Patch believed that it's a terrible indictment of who we have become, that some grow rich off the illnesses of others. And yet, this is the accepted practice in our nation and beyond. But the medical community need not be singled out, as they are not the exception, but the rule. Virtually all of us are operating under the same get-what-you-can-off-anyone-you-can philosophy. Whether in the grocery or garment industry, in education or entertainment, we are all encouraged, even expected, to charge the highest price for a good or service the market will bear. Yes, a doctor makes a profit off the ailments of people, but is it any different to make a profit off of feeding people? What about clothing people? What about educating them? And what about art, which is the nourishment of the soul? *"But people have a right to make a living,"* one might rightly object. Yes, of course—it's good and right to make a living. The objection raised here is not about making a living, it's about making a killing.

In his blistering essay "Rain and the Rhinoceros," Thomas Merton castigates western civilization for the commoditization of virtually everything. He writes:

Let me say this before rain becomes a utility that they can plan and distribute for money. By "they" I mean the people who cannot understand that rain is a festival, who do not appreciate its gratuity, who think that what has no price has no value, that what cannot be sold is not real, so that the only way to make something actual is to place it on the market. The time will come when they will sell you even your rain. At the moment it is still free, and I am in it.

It turns out that Merton's prediction was not so futuristic and farfetched. In fact, in 1999, a corporation based in San Francisco claimed ownership of all water rights in Cochabamba, Bolivia—even privatizing rainwater. Imagine committing a crime for opening your mouth and drinking the rain. In Cochabamba, you didn't have to imagine it; it was reality, until the citizenry rose up and revolted against this transcontinental tyranny. Most of us, too, would view this kind of privatization objectionable, and yet, when we consider the accepted premise of ownership in our own lives, is there not a troubling parallel? How is it fundamentally different when a landowner claims the rights to all water found on his or her property, say in a spring, lake, or stream? Where, after all, does this water come from, if not the rain? And if you can exclusively own such gross quantities of water, the origins of which no individual had anything to do with (also true of the land on which we find the water), is it so radically different to own the air, the sky, and eventually, the sunshine?

Native Americans found the notion of ownership preposterous and hence offered Manhattan in a trade with the Dutch, not because they were ignorant, but because they couldn't conceive of land being owned by anyone. When the Dutch gifted $24 worth of trinkets to the Lenni Lenape Indians, one of the tribes that lived on the island now known as Manhattan, the Lenape in exchange offered to share the land with the Dutch. The Dutch, however, assumed the exchange made them the exclusive owners, so they walled off the lower portion of the island to keep the Indians out. Shortly thereafter, the British seized the land, tore down the wall, and built a road, which became known as Wall Street. Isn't it interesting, if not prophetic, that Wall Street, now considered the focal point of greed and all that has gone wrong with the world's way of doing business, has a history based on a claim of exclusivity and ownership?

Ownership and commoditization may help us organize and structure our social agreements—I know where you live, what's "yours," and thereby respect those boundaries—but they are insidious bedfellows commanding us to put a price on what is originally and essentially a gift. It's what I did when I raised my rate into the multimillion-dollar stratosphere. It's important to note that raising one's rate does not happen automatically with commercial success. Believe me, no one runs up to you and offers you this amount of money. You have to ask for it; and ask for it, I did. And what's underneath the asking is a troubling assumption—that I am worth more; that I, Tom Shadyac, possess a unique talent, a goose that can lay a golden egg, and therefore deserve a disproportionate take from the gross resources garnered from a picture. I am more valuable than the cook, the drivers, the electricians, and the extras, so the studio must pay me more. This, of course, flies in the face of our widely accepted moral beliefs that we are all in this together, brothers and sisters, equal in the eyes of God. But the economic game we play lays waste to morality by conveniently proclaiming buying and selling the ultimate reality, and taking advantage of each other the norm. *"That's just business"* becomes the mindless mantra, allowing us to compartmentalize our lives, proclaiming love the highest aim on Sunday and monetary gain the penultimate on Monday. Yes, Jesus walked as a poor man among the poor, but he wants you to have it all! Sure, he commanded us not to worry about tomorrow, or even to store into barns, but is it so wrong to want to own the darn barn? Jesus certainly had a talent for teaching, but somehow he refrained from charging for his speeches. Either he was one lousy businessman, or he was on to a moral principle that deserves our consideration. Jesus knew his ability was a gift—he said he could do nothing without the Father who strengthened him—and therefore he did not claim ownership of his life and art.

✳

"Now art glorifies the artist affirming the part above the whole. That is why art too, serves death." This difficult and disturbing truth from Thomas Klise's classic novel, *The Last Western*, illuminates our culture's toxic tendency to elevate the artist, pay him untold sums of money, and thereby separate him from the source of his art, from people, injustice, the human condition,

the beauty of life. Consider the movie business, where we glorify the actor, the writer, the director, hold them up as gods and award them millions for their talent and services. But isn't all artistic genius a product of listening? Pulitzer Prize–winning poet Mary Oliver says she doesn't write poetry, she takes dictation and dresses it up a bit. Here, she is articulating what may be a bottom-line truth about the artistic process: It has more to do with openly receiving, than willfully generating. Like a radio station tuned to the right frequency, a gifted artist, inventor, or entrepreneur receives a kind of signal that comes in the form of an idea, a song, a poem, or a story. Examples are endless: Paul McCartney woke up with the lyrics of "Yesterday"; the idea for *Harry Potter,* according to J.K. Rowling, *"fell into her head"; Frankenstein* came to Mary Shelley in a dream, as did *Dr. Jekyll and Mr. Hyde* to Robert Louis Stevenson; even Albert Einstein, then a 26-year-old patent clerk, said of his theory of relativity that *"the breakthrough came suddenly."* Of course, much hard work, discipline, research, and reflection is required to create the climate for inspiration, but inspiration is, by definition, a gift. I know that I have never *thought* of a good idea in my life. I have *received* many good ideas. Isn't that why we use the term "gifted" in the first place? Emerson echoes this belief in his essay, *Spiritual Laws,* when he says: *"Men of an extraordinary success, in their honest moments, have always sung, 'Not unto us, not unto us.'"*

So the question arises, can I lay claim to any such gifts; can I say in truth that I *own* the art and inspiration that comes through me? Wendell Berry articulates this challenge in his indicting poem, "Some Further Words":

> *Nor do I believe*
> *"artistic genius" is the possession*
> *of any artist. No one has made*
> *the art by which one makes the works*
> *of art. Each one who speaks speaks*
> *as a convocation. We live as councils*
> *of ghosts. It is not "human genius"*
> *that makes us human, but an old love,*
> *an old intelligence of the heart*
> *we gather to us from the world,*
> *from the creatures, from the angels*
> *of inspiration, from the dead*

Berry does not mince words regarding the poison that has infected commerce when he writes:

> *"Intellectual property" names*
> *the deed by which the mind is bought*
> *and sold, the world enslaved. We*
> *who do not own ourselves, being free,*
> *own by theft what belongs to God,*
> *to the living world, and equally*
> *to us all.*

So, what exactly do I "own" of my art? Is it just and right that I reap whatever rewards I can get, or is there a more balanced approach, one that reflects the true nature of art's inception and source?

Dialogue Seventeen:

FEAR: Ah, so now I see what this has been all along, a rallying cry against ownership.

TRUTH: I have no such intention. I only wish to pose the question, *Who can really own anything?* When Jonas Salk invented the polio vaccine, he was asked, *"Who owns the patent?"* His response was simply, *"There is no patent. Can you patent the sun?"*

FEAR: So he didn't want to get rich; that's his problem.

TRUTH: He did get rich. He saved millions of lives. All because he refused to attach a single poisonous word to his work.

FEAR: What word is that?

TRUTH: What do you call the land you live on? You say, *"This land's not yours it's . . ."?*

FEAR: Mine!

TRUTH: And when you dig a hole in the ground and plunder the earth for metals you call precious, you call this a . . . ?

FEAR: Mine.

TRUTH: And what do you call a device that explodes under your feet, a device that maims, cripples, and kills? This is known as a . . . ?

FEAR: Mine.

TRUTH: And this killing occurs because someone felt *"this land is not yours it's . . ."?*

FEAR: Mine!

TRUTH: Do you see a pattern here? This game you are playing is exhausting you. I simply ask why you do not put it down and rest.

FEAR: This game is how we eat. It's how we survive!

TRUTH: Then is it not wise to examine the values on which it is based? Perhaps you will finally see the tail you are chasing is your own.

FEAR: Don't you get it? What I am chasing is survival!

TRUTH: And you are so caught up in the chase, you are unaware of how severely it has blinded you. This is the problem, Fear: *you run our current economy, and your philosophy is unwise, unsustainable, and will inevitably lead to man's demise.*

FEAR: My philosophy is reality. I say don't just take what you need, take whatever you can get. And yes, charge the highest price you can for your talent, for a good or service. If the market will bear it, you'd be an idiot not to ask for it.

TRUTH: So let's apply this take-whatever-you-can philosophy to the workings of the human body.

FEAR: What are you talking about?

TRUTH: If a philosophy is sound, it should be applicable to any living system. And the human body is a living system, is it not?

FEAR: Of course it is.

TRUTH: So, according to your philosophy and under the current economic laws, an individual is to charge as much as possible for a good or service. On a movie set, the director is often the most valuable and can therefore charge the most. So what are the "directors" of the human body? What are the most valuable parts?

FEAR: Well, the brain, of course.

TRUTH: But the brain needs two things to function, oxygen and blood. Where do these come from?

FEAR: The heart and the lungs.

TRUTH: Right. Nothing works in the body without the heart and lungs. So let's give the heart and lungs "ownership" of the products they distribute, the blood and the oxygen. And since we know the heart and lungs are valuable, they can charge a very high price for their product, for their services. Now, what do you think would happen in the human body if the heart only sent blood to the organs that could afford its price or if the lungs refused to distribute oxygen without proper payment?

FEAR: It's obvious what would happen.

TRUTH: Yes, the body would die. If the heart and lungs behaved as people now behave, the brain that you said was so valuable would shut down. The organs would starve.

(A long pause . . . .)

FEAR: This is not a fair analogy. The human body is one organism. The economy is made up of millions of separate people.

TRUTH: And now we have come to the essential question: Are those people really separate? Isn't science now discovering the opposite? Haven't the mystics and their moral teachings told us the same for millennia, that everything is one?

FEAR: Do not bring up the mystics and their morality when talking science. Morality and the way things work do not belong together!

TRUTH: Don't you see? Morality *is* the way things work.

(Another long pause . . . .)

FEAR: It's just too hard to accept. Morality is morality. Science is science.

TRUTH: And yet, after centuries of disparity, are they not now coming together? Has science not recently discovered in the lab what the mystics have long intuited in the heart—that all matter is connected, that all humans beings are one family?

FEAR: Fine, there is a parallel. But this parallel cannot walk in the real world. Men will never see beyond their separation; they will never give up the idea of owning things!

TRUTH: It is not about owning things, but understanding the illusory nature of that ownership, of that division.

FEAR: And if we do understand? What then?

TRUTH: Our hearts open as the prophet foretold: "The heart and soul of all men being one, this bitterness of *His* and *Mine* ceases. His is mine. I am my brother and my brother is me."

FEAR: This is about our brotherhood?

TRUTH: This is about who you are.

FEAR: I am my brother?

TRUTH: And my brother is me.

FEAR: All things are one.

TRUTH: You are beginning to see.

THE RICHEST MAN IN TOWN

✳

It is one of the most beautiful compensations
of life that no man can sincerely try to help
another without helping himself . . .
Serve and thou shalt be served.

—RALPH WALDO EMERSON

The best way to find yourself,
is by losing yourself in the service of others.

—MAHATMA GANDHI

IT HAS BEEN SAID BY MY CRITICS that I wish to bring down capitalism. I do not. Jesus did not preach a new system, but an ancient truth, the truth that love heals all. And so I propose that love, when applied to capitalism in the form of compassion and empathy, will cover a multitude of sins. In fact, compassion and capitalism have coexisted quite well before. The most obvious examples lay in the world of nonprofits, all of which by definition run on a different value set but still operate inside our current economic system. These groups stand boldly outside the societal stampede, consciously choosing people over profits, and define wealth not as money stockpiled, but as love shared in its many forms: a meal delivered, medicine given, a seed planted, creativity inspired, a helping hand extended. St. Jude Children's Research Hospital in Memphis, Tennessee, is one such organization. This miraculous institution runs on a simple philosophy: No cancer-stricken child should be denied treatment, regardless of ability to pay. Traditional profits do not interest St. Jude, but rather, St. Jude calls it most profitable to serve those in need for free. Since its founding in 1962, no one has ever paid a nickel for treatment, whether you are from the wealthiest family or the poorest. The business world would call that insane; St. Jude calls it natural and right.

My father, a lawyer in the Washington, DC area, helped build the hospital and ran it for 13 years, taking a significant pay cut from his lucrative law practice. In fact, most doctors at St. Jude could make more money elsewhere, but they choose a different kind of wealth, in open opposition to the pay-me-more mantra of modern-day society. One only need walk the hospital's campus to feel the power of this compassionate mission. *"Law is what I did,"* my father often said, *"but St. Jude is who I am."* And yet, he also said it was naïve to believe such a model could be replicated with regularity. He felt it was unrealistic to imagine more of these altruistic institutions emerging because, in his words, "it's not who people are." Strange, because he stated plainly that St. Jude is who he was. Strange, because he did the very thing he believed we were incapable of: he built a hugely successful business that gives its product away for free.

St. Jude is, in fact, a perfect example of the economy of nature—*it freely receives, and it freely gives.* It need not be the exception, but a lightning rod, pointing the way to a more sustainable and equitable future. And since happiness is found not in greater sums of money but in a greater measure of meaning, is this model not indicating a more effective approach to business and to life?*

✳

THE DOCUMENTARY *I AM* begins with a haunting quote from Einstein: *"Humanity is going to require a substantially new way of thinking in order to survive."* If that statement was coming from Butch Einstein, the deli owner on Pico and Third, it'd be one thing; but it's coming from Albert Einstein, arguably the greatest mind of the 20th century. That means your kids and my kids might not be around to have kids. The thought is sobering. And notice, Einstein is specifically calling for *a new way of thinking.* He's not talking about a law that needs to be passed or trading one system for another; he's asking us to reconsider the mind-set that undergirds everything we do—the way we educate, approach business, and treat the natural world. So what might this new way of thinking be?

Consider that the world of the future will operate under a very simple premise: *we're going to serve each other.* What we now label as *non*—nonprofits, nonviolence, nongovernmental agencies—are actually the opposite, the way forward, the way to *pro*gress. Competition will no longer be our god. We will cease

---

* Author's note: Because of St. Jude's powerful example, I now operate my entertainment company, Shady Acres, essentially as a nonprofit. (I laugh at the term *nonprofit,* as serving others is infinitely profitable!) We will still tell stories that move, enlighten, and entertain, but any and all after-tax profits will be returned to the common good. The documentary *I AM* was our first nonprofit venture. Everyone on *I AM* was paid a salary according to their needs. Needs include the staples of life and the exploration of a passion, be it the purchase of a bike or a canvas to create art. All other proceeds flow back out.

having to beat each other, and actually and practically embrace the idea that we are all in this together, brothers and sisters, one tribe. Businesses will be built that reflect our belief that love is the highest aim. Starbucks will become Ourbucks; U.S. Airways will become Us Airways; and Bank of America really will *be* the Bank of America. Someone's going to do it; someone's going to turn Walmart into Allmart. Imagine it: rather than concentrating billions in the hands of one family, Allmart's money is used to educate children, feed the hungry, house the homeless, heal the natural world, and uplift local communities. Who would take on such a task? Who wouldn't? How blessed will an individual truly be who sees this altruistic vision through to fruition, and thereby becomes, like George Bailey at the end of *It's a Wonderful Life*, the richest man in town?

We all have the power to participate in this transformation, regardless of income. If the poor still secretly envy the rich, they will add to the energy that keeps things as they are. Our reactions must become like that of certain native and indigenous peoples, who, when they came upon the equivalent of a billionaire, said, *"Oh, I'm sorry to hear that."* As Emerson reminds us:

Men such as they are, very naturally seek money or power . . . And why not? for they aspire to the highest, and this, in their sleep-walking, they dream is highest. Wake them and they shall quit the false good and leap to the true . . .

And it is just that, a matter of waking up, of blinking away the sleep dust of a drowsy culture and opening our eyes to what is real—not what we presently call reality, this story we've been telling ourselves that we are all separate, this me-first mantra that puts up an illusory wall between brothers and sisters, between human beings and the natural world. If you've ever seen a good hypnotist, you know he or she can make people do all kinds of irrational things. Through the power of suggestion, a mesmerist can control your thoughts and hence, your behavior, making otherwise calm and collected volunteers cluck like chickens and bark like dogs. Many of us are still such volunteers, not on the carnival stage but on the stage of life, lulled to sleep by a misanthropic message, cajoled into behaviors that have us howling at the moon, unaware. *Love is the highest aim* can no longer exist aside *Give me more!* The morality of Jesus and Wall Street are not reconcilable. Mr. Buffett may have amassed billions, but the moral imperative is not, *What would Warren do?* No economy exists outside of the citizens who fuel it; no corporation has any power we don't give it. The Occupy Wall Street movement is currently protesting corporate power, expressing the collective outrage at the all-too-pervasive greed-is-good mentality. But it is not enough to be *against* something, we must be *for* something. Have we not spent enough time pointing out the splinter in our brother's eye, ignoring the plank in our own? When enough of us heal the greed in our own hearts, Wall Street and Washington will come around. For they are not our leaders in Congress, they are our followers. Let's give them something to follow. Let's sweep and clean floors, as Emerson urges, with the effulgent day beams of God bursting forth, and make all others want to grab mops and brooms. We can no longer afford to simply listen to the Sunday sermon; we must become the sermon. For it is love and love alone that breaks down all barriers; love alone shatters all walls, even walls built in homage to false gods, even walls that have streets named after them.

Dialogue Eighteen:

FEAR: You speak of a Pollyanna world where we are going to serve each other. But why do you ignore what our business leaders have done to advance humanity? They have done as much as our moral leaders, and perhaps more.
TRUTH: This is what you believe?

FEAR: Of course. And I am not alone. A few years ago, there was a commercial from a computer giant that said the same. The ad intercut images of business leaders with moral leaders. The ad ended with the company's slogan, *Think different.* Do you know the commercial?
TRUTH: Yes. The commercial said to think different, but it is very much about thinking the same.

FEAR: What are you talking about? Our business leaders are revolutionaries. They moved the human race forward, just like the ad says.
TRUTH: So you believe when a businessman creates a product, the human race is moved forward?

FEAR: Look at what these people came up with—new airlines, new computers, new media outlets! We can access information with the click of a button. We can travel at high speeds. We have products developed daily that make our lives easier.

TRUTH: So moving faster is moving forward? More convenience equals more happiness?

FEAR: I know what the studies say, that none of these things make us happier. Well, I don't believe them!

TRUTH: If moving faster and more material things move us forward, why do our moral leaders, the same moral leaders in this very commercial, encourage us to slow down? To be empty and thus be full? To "be still, and know that I am God"?

FEAR: Are you saying this progress is not progress? That these inventions are bad?!

TRUTH: They are not bad and they are not good. What matters is the *value* brought to these inventions.

FEAR: You have said this before. That technology is neutral. It is not neutral. Technology connects people.

TRUTH: And what connects us, disconnects us, as well. A student connects to another through texting—a gain—but ignores the world around him, the sun setting in the distance, his fellow student in his presence—a cost. Cost and gain, this is the law . . . Are you aware of the prevalence of Internet bullying?

FEAR: Here you go again, pointing out the negative. Not everything about technology can be positive.

TRUTH: And this is the point: before we can say whether something moves us forward, is it not wise to define what *moving forward* means?

FEAR: So define it: what moves the human race forward?

TRUTH: What is it that we have seen at the root of how life thrives?

FEAR: You repeat this over and over.

TRUTH: It bears repeating. On what principle does life thrive?

FEAR: Cooperation.

TRUTH: And cooperation is rooted in what value?

FEAR: Don't tell me this is about love again? Love moves us forward?

TRUTH: Whatever compels the human species to act in a more loving and compassionate way, whatever truly connects us, yes, does indeed move us forward.

FEAR: You don't think these businessmen in the commercial fit your definition? You don't think they have promoted love and compassion and moved us forward?

TRUTH: The commercial does not allude to the love and compassion these businessmen may have added to the world. *Your* suggestion is that their business accomplishments alone move us forward; and I do not accept that premise.

FEAR: You cannot tell me these inventions have not moved us forward! Look at the car. Yes, it can be used to rob a bank, but overall, it is good. It is a net positive.

TRUTH: Is it a positive that the car has added pollution to our air, caused wars over the use of oil, disrupted the silence and sounds of nature with its roar, killed and maimed millions, and contributed to obesity as its use surged and walking declined?

FEAR: Again, you point out only the negative. If a woman has a heart attack in a restaurant and she is saved, two pieces of technology come into play: the cell phone and the ambulance. The cell phone dials the hospital. The ambulance moves the patient.

TRUTH: But it was not simply the cell phone and the ambulance. It was compassion that made the citizen dial the phone. It was love that made the ambulance driver drive. A value was added to both that now has you saying technology moves humanity forward.

FEAR: But the ambulance was needed and so was the cell phone!

TRUTH: Imagine 200 years from now: Humanity, through its own genius, does itself in. Perhaps we warm the planet, or release a virus from a lab, or set off a nuclear holocaust. If an alien being wishes to recount what happened to the human race, would he say technology moved us forward or killed us off?

FEAR: I know what you want me to say.

TRUTH: Only what happened in this scenario. Only what is true.

FEAR: In this scenario, technology killed us off.

TRUTH: So it is not technology alone that moves us forward. *It is the value that is added to our technology that is critical.* Do you see this now?

(A long pause . . . .)

FEAR: It's hard to admit. But, yes.

TRUTH: And what value moves us forward?

FEAR: I cannot bring myself to say it.

TRUTH: Then look around you—it is written everywhere, in all of creation.

FEAR: It's too simple. Love can't be what moves us forward. What about education? Doesn't education move us forward?

TRUTH: When it is rooted in love, yes. But our schools now bow to a false god and presently suffer the pains of that idolatry.

FEAR: More exaggeration. Our schools need work, but overall they are fine; they are good.

TRUTH: In other words, you would like to remain in charge of them.

FEAR: I bring practicality to education. When people are afraid they work harder.

TRUTH: If hard work is the answer, why are so many of our schools failing? It is a question you do not dare to ask.

FEAR: This is a waste of time. And I have no interest in your inquiry.

TRUTH: Then, like always, close your eyes, Fear. But I am still compelled to ask, *what has gone wrong with our system of education?*

EDUCA-SHUN

*

*To free the mind from the habit of competition,
we must see in detail the process by
which the mind is ensnared by competition.*

—MARGUERITE BEECHER

*Education is what remains when one has forgotten
everything he learned in school.*

—ALBERT EINSTEIN

THERE'S A LOT ONE CAN LEARN from a snow day. Yes, there's the joyful experience of a blessed day of play—and blessed by the authorities, nonetheless!—but there's also something telling in the unbridled glee at escaping the chain link and linoleum life that is school. Adulthood offers nothing that compares. Oprah has her giveaways, but the madness of instant gratification goes as quick as it comes; a day of play hits us kids deep. But what is it about that chain link and what goes on inside of it that a simple snow day has us feeling as if we've just escaped Shawshank and, like Andy Dufresne, are finally bursting out of the sewer pipes to freedom?

There is little doubt and less debate; our schools need help. Democrat or Republican, liberal or conservative, bring up the topic and walls fall, deep-rooted divisions vanish, and near universal agreement rings out: *"Something must be done!"* But what exactly? Here, our united front divides and differing opinions offer differing solutions. *"It's money! Our schools need more money!"* is the most common cry of the would-be reformers. But is money really a panacea? Exactly what amount of it will lower students' stress levels, now at record highs, or keep our kids from bullying each other? And what check could be written that would lift a child out of depression or eliminate a youth's addiction to mood-altering medications? If money is a cure-all, why did Jesus kick over the moneylenders' tables? Would it not have been better to keep them upright and ask for a handout?

Some even go so far as to say academia is suffering because we have outlawed prayer in our public schools. *"God's wrath is upon us! The Lord has been removed from the classroom, and therefore, His blessing has been removed, as well!"* At first glance, this kind of fearmongering is foolhardy and posits an impossibility: God cannot be removed from our schools any more than He can be siphoned from a sunset, a stream, or a wildflower. *"Omnipresence is not just a rumor,"* as Hafiz reminds us. True, you can keep a child from reciting the Lord's Prayer, but are our children not living prayers? When a student is kind to a classmate, is that not *Thy kingdom come?* When a student expresses gratitude to a cafeteria worker, is that not *on earth as it is in heaven?* Whatever the prayer policy in our public schools, the sublime scripture remains irrevocable: *"Christ is all in all."* But here's where the zealot's cry has unintended merit: The principles on which our educational system is rooted, *competition and winning,* dim God's light in our schools, by dimming His light in our students. Our children do not sit across from a brother or sister to be encouraged, but a foe to be conquered. We are teaching a Divine opposite: students must defeat one another, not love one another; they must win at all costs, not be compassionate at all times. What propels our system forward pulls the love of God backward.

I speak from experience as a winner at this game, or should I say, a loser. As a student, I was not just to do my best, but to *be* the best. If any of us fail at this academic ascent, the consequences are dire: scholastic doors close, employment opportunities wither, and we, the losers, are shut out from society's succor; we may not eat. Is it any wonder, under this do-or-die pressure, that some kids break? I recently spoke to a group of Pepperdine University law students who said they are discouraged from helping one another with their studies. This from a school founded on the teachings of Jesus who, as I recall, did not say, *"faith, hope, and competition, but the greatest of these is competition!"* But Jesus did not live in today's world, or so the argument goes; *"Why should I help you, when that help may prevent me from helping myself?"* This kind of deluded logic is yesterday's story, based on the false assumption that there is a "me" that has no connection to "you." Thankfully, Martin Luther King, Jr. was not ruled by Pepperdine's law, but God's law, when he said: *"I can never be what I ought to be until you are what you ought to be. And you can never be what you ought to be until I am what I ought to be. This is the interrelated structure of reality."*

But today's academic pressures have traded this structure of reality for a ladder of exclusivity, where students are taught to climb over each other in a race to the top. Is it any surprise that bullying flourishes in this hothouse environment? Recently, a

Rutgers freshman was the victim of a heartless bullying prank. The twisted joke began when his roommate filmed the teenager in an intimate act with another boy, then posted the tryst online. Humiliated and embarrassed, the young man took his own life by jumping off the George Washington Bridge. School officials were outraged and quickly moved to prosecute the cruel and insensitive roommate. But where was the prosecution of the cruel and insensitive system that pits student against student? Where was the investigation into the atmosphere created by a society that rewards being number one over being benevolent? Bullying does not occur in a vacuum; it's a fruit sprouting from the seeds we sow. And what are those seeds? *Separate yourself from the pack, be number one, take care of yourself first, and win.* But winning and beating each other are just one step removed from teasing and berating each other. And bullying doesn't stop there. Our society has seen an unprecedented rise in the number of school shootings, where children as young as six years old, their anger and isolation reaching a boiling point, bring guns to schools and leave bloodbaths in their wake.

As terrible and tragic as these school shootings are, if we trace them back, we find logic, albeit a twisted logic, at their root: it is competition taken to its extreme. *"I have been taught to compete and win. I cannot win in the traditional way. I will win in my own twisted way."* Note that school shootings do not show up in native, indigenous, or traditional societies. Tibetan children do not kill one other. Nor do youth in Bhutan, Nepal, or Ladakh. Why would they? They are encouraged to be as compassionate as the Dalai Lama, not as competitive as Michael Jordan. No society outside our current cultural paradigm is infected with these kinds of adolescent mass murders. Ours is—not because of bad luck or some cosmic accident, but because we stubbornly cling to a warped ideology, that competition is the ruling order of nature, that it is the highest ideal.

Even the U.S. Department of Education is full of the present-day poison when it states its goal clearly: *"to promote student achievement and preparation for global competitiveness."* This isn't the objective of a Fortune 500 company; this is the mission statement on education from our own government. Forgive my directness, but has a shallower aspiration ever been declared? Is being number one in the global marketplace really our highest hope for our children? Do our elected officials really believe that winning is an elixir that produces happiness and contentment among our students and citizens? Positive psychology, the field that studies contentment, has proven again and again that competitive prowess and happiness have little to do with each other. A few short years ago, when America ranked number one in the world in college graduates, we were nowhere near number one in happiness. We're still number one economically and militarily, but again, our nation is nowhere near the happiest. The evidence has been gathered but has yet to sink in; it is the intrinsic, the internal, and not the extrinsic, or external, that improves the quality of life. *What matters is who we are, not who we beat.*

But modern-day education espouses the opposite and has our kids in daily competition for the best grades, the best SAT scores, the best AP classes, and the best graduate and professional schools—all with the implied idea that these will lead to the best life. I partook fully in this stress fest, winning at the grade game—I pulled a 3.8 in college—but losing at the game of life. I slept little, my health suffered, and I drank heavily to numb out. It's no secret that most college students drink and many use drugs, but what remains a mystery is why. Is it just innocent experimentation, or is it an indication of something deeper, a fundamental flaw in the system we force our students into? John Lennon hit the Rusty Nail on the head when he said:

The basic thing nobody asks is, why do people take drugs of any sort? . . . Why do we have these accessories to normal living to live? I mean, is there something wrong with society that's making us so pressurized, that we cannot live without guarding ourselves against it?

And these stresses are not decreasing, but increasing. The grading scale, for example, no longer stops at 4.0; it now ascends to 4.5 and beyond, with that much more ladder to climb up. The effects on our students are chilling. A recent MSNBC report revealed 50 percent of college students have at one point considered suicide. That's *50 percent.* Half of our "best and brightest" entertain the thought of killing themselves to relieve this intense academic pressure. Is this not a loud enough alarm? Must we wait for half of our children to go through with the act?

Understand, this is not a call to eliminate competition; there is merit in its reasonable exercise. But we have gone far beyond reasonable; we have warped competition's original intent. Competition derives from the Latin word, *competere*, meaning *to strive with.* Thus, rival athletes, Bjorn Borg and John McEnroe, Magic Johnson and Larry Bird, *strove with* one other, elevating each other's talents to new heights. When I study the films of

Steven Spielberg, Bob Zemeckis, Peter Weir, and Danny Boyle, I am pulled upward and out, expanded in my art and perspective, *striving with* their genius to serve the art that moves through me. But our culture does not encourage us to simply strive with; we must win, *win at all costs, win or die trying.* And herein lies the toxicity; we have attached a life-or-death value to victory, an eighth deadly sin, which is: *to the winner belong the spoils.* We know it all too well, the athlete signing the multimillion-dollar contract, the CEO cashing the seven-figure bonus check. The warped message reaches our students at the earliest age: the winner gets it all, the loser gets in line.

Most recognize the injustice but accept it as a part of life—the cleanup hitter making $250 million while the inner-city teacher can barely feed her family. But the athlete does not deserve to be singled out any more than the businessman, the doctor, the lawyer, or even the artist, who passively accepts this fatal philosophy and passes it on to the next generation. *Be number one or be gone.* This is what we teach our kids. Is it any wonder they are stressed out and suicidal? Is it any wonder their hopes wane, their hearts weaken, their spirits list? When competition is elevated to such heights, do we not see that fight or flight is the natural response? For every 100 that compete, 99 lose. Is this the kind of world we want to leave our children? *"If I saw a competitor drowning I'd put a live fire hose in his mouth,"* boasted McDonald's founder, Ray Kroc. What student would not be shaken by this ideology? Do we not see this is the real junk food we are feeding our children—do unto others *before* they do unto you? Tragically, unaware, we have rewritten the golden rule and made it only about gold.

But even the elevation of competition pales in comparison to the real tragedy of modern education. What is this tragedy, and how does it affect, even suppress, the unique talents and gifts that animate our children?

Dialogue Nineteen:

FEAR: I see nothing wrong with rewarding the winners of competitions.
TRUTH: Then reward them with praise for their excellence, with appreciation for their gifts.

FEAR: And what's wrong with giving them money? As you said, to the victor belong the spoils.
TRUTH: A spoil is *"plunder taken from an enemy in war or from a victim in robbery."* Is this the kind of society we wish to build—a society based on war, based on robbery?

FEAR: It is not robbery. It is victory! The victor obeyed the rules and won! Besides, it has always been this way.
TRUTH: It has not always been this way. Native cultures did not grant the fastest runner or the best hunter a disproportionate take of the tribe's resources.

FEAR: But the athlete works hard and deserves what he gets. So does the artist. So does the doctor!
TRUTH: Does the athlete work harder than the maintenance man hauling trash, the police officer patrolling gang territory,

the migrant worker picking lettuce, the deployed soldier fighting society's battles? Could an argument not be made that the athlete or artist, blessed with pursuing his or her passion for sport and art, make *less* than the sanitation worker shouldering the burden of cleaning toilets and maintaining sewers?

FEAR: Now you are being ridiculous.
TRUTH: So it is ridiculous to regard the labor of others as valuable?

FEAR: The athlete has a limited window to make money. He can't always be the fastest. The artist cannot always be the most relevant.
TRUTH: And why then, when the athlete slows and the artist loses relevancy, can't he or she begin to teach or serve in the local community?

FEAR: Because these things don't pay as much!
TRUTH: Do you not see that these jobs don't pay as much because the athlete and artist are disproportionately rewarded in the first place? There is nothing left to pay the teacher and the social worker.

FEAR: Your vision is unrealistic. Excellence should be celebrated. Winners should be celebrated.
TRUTH: Celebrated yes, not elevated.

FEAR: What does any of this have to do with education?
TRUTH: It has everything to do with education. With every check written, society teaches its children what it values.

FEAR: But I see nothing wrong with the mentality that exists in our system. The winners get A's, get into the best schools, and are rewarded with scholarships and the best jobs. The message is clear and motivates students.

TRUTH: And what is the message sent to the losers?

FEAR: That they have lost! Society can't take care of everyone.

TRUTH: One way or another, society will reckon with every one of its members. *"He who has a thousand friends has not a friend to spare. And he who has one enemy shall meet him everywhere."*

FEAR: So those who don't win turn into society's enemies?

TRUTH: What is a criminal after all but someone who is hungry?

FEAR: What? Criminals don't just steal to eat.

TRUTH: And hunger does not just mean an absence of food.

FEAR: So what—they are hungry for meaning?

TRUTH: They are hungry for what we are all hungry for.

FEAR: Oh, please! Every point you make boils down to love.

TRUTH: It is how things work.

FEAR: Even education?

TRUTH: Especially education.

THE GOSPEL OF THOMAS

✳

I'm not a teacher, but an awakener.

—ROBERT FROST

*The fact is . . . education doesn't need
to be reformed—it needs to be transformed.*

—SIR KEN ROBINSON

FOR MUCH OF MY LIFE, I was convinced I was dumb. This isn't self-loathing or low self-esteem talking; it's the conclusion I reached from my experience in our school system. Sure, I was able to post above-average grades, but these were achieved after countless hours of study, of working and reworking any and all assignments. Virtually nothing came easy; I plodded through homework problems, word, math, or otherwise; I read slowly, backtracking often until sentences sunk into the concrete I was sure was my mind. And while I labored, beside me the true geniuses tap-danced through the curriculum with Fred Astaire ease. If only I could glide through science like David Nelson, or waltz through math like Peter Jones. School had taught me to compare—and by comparison, I had two left feet.

But sophomore year of high school brought a glimmer of hope when an English teacher handed out a unique creative writing assignment: we were to write a monologue bringing an inanimate object to life and then act out those monologues in front of the class. I became a fork in a dishwasher cycle, and holding both hands high, told some jokes about smelling my armpits and dealing with inclement weather: *"One minute it's raining, the next it's hot and dry. How's a utensil supposed to dress for this?!"* It was not the usual, soul-sucking scholastic exercise I was forced to complete. I found myself fully engaged, energized, excited by the challenge. *"No one need force me to do this,"* was the unfamiliar thought circling in my head. *"I like doing this!"* You see, throughout my education, joy and learning had become mutually exclusive; a child could experience one or the other but not both simultaneously. But somehow, with this playful exercise, oil and water coalesced; learning and joy became one and the same.

It would not be until my fifth year of college that those strange bedfellows would reunite. Needing just one credit to graduate, I took a writing and directing class outside of my major, in the theater department at the University of Virginia, and the heavens parted for a second time. This wasn't just a class; it was a door opening in front of me, *in* me. I came alive, acting, writing, telling jokes, directing scenes; homework assignments were no longer dreaded, they were opportunities to create. My scholastic struggles disappeared; there was an ease in the midst of the work—and there was lots of work!— that felt natural and right. I didn't have a thought about what grade I'd get, and yet, I not only received an A, I was singled out for my creativity and sense of humor. Looking back, I realize now I wasn't dumb after all. My struggles were not based on a lack of ability or intelligence; they were rooted in what I'd been taught and how I'd been taught. My schooling was the famous parable come to life: *I was a fish who'd been asked to climb a tree.*

Educator Sir Ken Robinson believes everyone has intelligence. Rather than asking, *are* you intelligent? Ken asks, *how* are you intelligent? It's a question we don't pose often enough; it's a question that goes right to the heart of what's wrong with education. In fact, it could be argued that *education* is not an accurate label for what our academic institutions actually do. Education is from the Latin word, *educare*, meaning *to draw out* or *bring out from within*. So when we educate in the truest sense, we are to draw out the talents and interests of our children. But ours is a system of conformity and standards; we do not *draw out* as much as *drill in. Schooling* is a more appropriate term—as we do indeed, *school* our children: we school them in math, in science, in history; we school them in mechanical disciplines and job skills, with little to no emphasis on life skills. We are not Socratic in our approach and do not ask our students to teach us about themselves that we may serve the light that is uniquely theirs. Instead, we tell our students, from the earliest age, what they need to know, and sadly, implied underneath, who they need to be. Famed Scottish author Muriel Spark observed this upside-down approach, saying:

To me education is a leading out of what is already there in the pupil's soul. To Miss Mackay it is a putting in of something that is not there, and that is not what I call education, I call it intrusion.

Intrusion. A strong word. But if what Miss Mackay *drills in* interferes with what education is meant to *draw out,* then perhaps not strong enough. The Gospel of Thomas puts it this way: *"If you bring forth that which is within you, that which is within you will save you. If you do not bring forth that which is within you, that which is within you will destroy you."* Here the stakes are made clear: true education becomes a matter of life and death—if not for the body, then for the soul and spirit. If you are a poet, and inside you words are calling out that can help heal, if that art is drawn out, you will beam with meaning and purpose; you will, as the gospel suggests, be saved. If those words stay stuck inside you, fermenting, if those words are not drawn out, the light that is in you, that *is* you, will fade; you will, as the gospel warns, be destroyed. The teacher trapped behind the accountant's desk, the artist suffocating in a cubicle—the Gospel of Thomas leaves no room for doubt: *these talents must come forth.*

But why don't they come forth? In *Walking on Water: Reflections on Faith and Art,* Madeleine L'Engle points out an alarming statistic: At the age of five, 90 percent of all children identify themselves as highly creative; by the time they are seven, just *two years after starting school,* that number drops to 10 percent; and when they reach adulthood, it is less than 2 percent. In just two short years after children are delivered into the hands of our educational system, their belief in their creative nature withers. Why? What is it about our approach to education that lays waste to the unique abilities of our youth?

✳

ALL CHILDREN ARE natural-born learners, entering this world boundlessly curious and inquisitive. Studies have confirmed this for decades, though simple observation is evidence enough: Children energetically explore whatever surrounds them, enthusiastically examine with touch, sight, sound, and smell, virtually any object within reach. They readily ask questions, seeking knowledge, soaking up any and all available information. But upon entering school, that boundless curiosity is bridled, their questioning nature quelled. Children are no longer free to explore, but are told to *"sit still," "be quiet," "pay attention,"* and *"stop staring out the window."* Their interest, of course, is drawn out that window, and rightly so, by the oak tree inviting them to climb, by the pile of leaves beckoning them to play. A teacher herself, poet Mary Oliver has seen the wide-eyed wonder of the preschooler transform by grade 12 into the lifeless stare of the high school senior. Thus, she has cryptically said, *"We are turning our children into the product."* Is it any wonder that in this country alone, 7,000 students drop out of school every day?

There is one basic question from which true education derives, a question the present-day system all too often fails to ask: *"Who are you?"* And from there, *"What do you love?"* No answer should be disregarded, even answers that point to play. If a student enjoys basketball, he or she can practice math from players' statistical analysis, science from the mechanics of a bouncing ball, and English from the literature surrounding the game. Wherever passion lies, whether surfing, cooking, painting, singing, writing, or drawing, learning naturally follows, unfolding easily without dampening enthusiasm for creativity and life. But far too many students are round pegs being pounded into square holes. Paul McCartney finished school without a single teacher recognizing his talent for music; Paulo Coelho was given shock therapy to discourage his writing; even Albert Einstein failed to flourish in traditional academia.

But the system's faults don't just affect the famous. For every Einstein, thousands become similarly discouraged. They are the extraordinary ordinary who are never asked the essential question: *"What makes you come alive?"* It is no accident. From kindergarten up, academia now seeks a singular outcome—train our kids for jobs, prepare them for the workplace. Just note the governor of Florida's latest vow to spend all new tax dollars solely on curriculums that lead to employment for students. Georgia schools now intend to require students to declare a career path by ninth grade, some as early as fifth grade. Does no one think it unreasonable that a ten-year-old decide what he is going to do for the rest of his life? I'm presently 53 and I'm still trying to figure that out. Thankfully, I was not schooled in Georgia, where I might have been held back in the fifth grade for 42 years! But isn't education more than just filling jobs? Recall the mission statement from the U.S. Department of Education, which remains: *"to promote student achievement and preparation for global competitiveness."* Not a word about students discovering themselves, their talents, or their passions; not a peep about developing as people, becoming more expansive in their minds, hearts, and spirits. The sign hung over the Temple of Apollo, *Know Thyself,* has become *Know Thy Job.* Our wise Greek ancestors, apparently not wise enough to embrace the job as life's primary end, chose knowledge of self, reality, and truth, as the aim of education. We have chosen employment and a paycheck. Do we not see our children suffer daily from this erroneous homage? If we must train our children for something, can we not train them for the most essential work of all—to love, to pay attention, to give daily praise? Emily Dickinson expressed her expansive view in her poem "I Dwell in Possibility" when she said:

> *For Occupation—This—*
> *The spreading wide my narrow Hands*
> *To gather Paradise.*

Education ought to be nothing less: an invitation to spread wide our narrow hands to gather paradise, to participate in the unfolding of that paradise, to honor the Will in our hearts, to walk as God walks, among us, in us, as us.

Dialogue Twenty:

FEAR: What you suggest, that people follow their hearts, that education draw out what people are passionate about, is not realistic.
TRUTH: Why not?

FEAR: Because it's not practical! Not everybody can be a violinist. Are you going to have a 1,000-seat violin section?
TRUTH: Perhaps more.

FEAR: You're being ridiculous. No orchestra can accommodate that.
TRUTH: Fear, your problem is that you think about what is and not what could be. You say there are too many people who desire

to play the violin. Do you think God is not aware of how many people wish to play the violin? If He can count the hairs on your head, can He not count the number of violinists? A person with a genuine passion for the violin has that passion because God Himself wants it expressed. God wants to experience a particular type of music through a particular person at a particular time and place. Should we not honor Him and each play our note?

FEAR: Do the math. It won't work. Who will scrub toilets? Who will wash windows?

TRUTH: All who understand the beauty of service will willingly share in these tasks. The lead violinist with a heart for his fellow man will insist on doing his part, as will the conductor and the ticket taker. When the artist opens up to the joy of serving others, it may prove difficult to return him to his canvas.

FEAR: Even if others agree to share in difficult tasks, too many people will want to be musicians, actors, writers, directors.

TRUTH: Let's suppose there are a great many with the violin on their hearts. Could not some work in the music industry, helping to coordinate concerts, bringing music to those who might otherwise not experience it? There are ways to participate in designing and manufacturing violins, managing travel for musicians, and so on. If the passion to play still exits, working musicians can from time to time, vacate their chairs to accommodate the dream of those with differing levels of talent.

FEAR: You don't get it. Parents don't want their kids to be violinists! They want them to get good paying jobs, to be able to be competitive in the global economy.

TRUTH: That is not what they want. It's what they have been trained to want.

FEAR: Trained to want?

TRUTH: Yes. It's a story they tell themselves, and they have forgotten that it is just a story.

FEAR: Enlighten me. What do they really want for their sons and daughters?

TRUTH: What we all want: to be loved, even more so, to love.

FEAR: You are wrong. What parents want for their kids is security. Parents want their kids to be able to take care of themselves. They want them to be independent.

TRUTH: No one is independent. No one.

FEAR: What are you talking about? Many have made it on their own, from nothing.

TRUTH: Really? Can you name one?

FEAR: I can name hundreds. Bill Gates, for example. He's completely independent.

TRUTH: Bill Gates is not independent.

FEAR: What? He's the richest man in the world!

TRUTH: And he is utterly dependent on others. He is dependent on millions to buy his products; he's dependent on thousands to design his products; he's dependent on more to transport and sell those products. Do you not see, Fear, that we are all dependent on each other? As infants, we are dependent on our mother's breast for milk. When we are weaned, we are dependent on nature for her bounty. As we grow, we are dependent on others to teach us language, skills, to pass on their knowledge. Fear, you are even dependent on me now, to have this conversation.

FEAR: Alright, you know what? I'm not afraid to say it: parents want their kids to have the finer things in life. I see nothing wrong with that.

TRUTH: We are finally in agreement. I will even go one step further; I want them to have the *finest* things in life. We will differ, of course, on what those things are. You will say it is cars, houses, retirement accounts, boats. I will say it is love, family, friendships, creativity, service, beauty.

FEAR: You know what your problem is? You live in a fantasy world. I live in the real world.

TRUTH: If anything I say is not reality at its core, please discard it immediately.

FEAR: You don't even want our schools to grade.

TRUTH: I don't know what grades mean.

FEAR: That's ridiculous. If a person is excellent in a subject, say math, they get an A. What's so hard to understand about that?
TRUTH: It tells me very little. How exactly are they excellent? Are they excellent at asking questions, thinking outside the box, at articulation, attitude, cooperation, leadership, flexibility? Do they work hard, exhibit passion, willingness, and kindness? What is the arc to their story? Are they growing, expanding, alive with curiosity? Or has life exacted a toll, dimming their spark and their light?

FEAR: What does all that have to do with math?
TRUTH: It has to do with life.

FEAR: The subject is math, not life.
TRUTH: I don't know how to separate the two.

FEAR: Math is addition and subtraction. Life is everything else.
TRUTH: So math is not a part of life?

FEAR: It's a skill. A grade just tells you if a person is good at that skill, that's all.
TRUTH: That's the point; it's not enough.

FEAR: But what if an employer just wants to know if a person can add?
TRUTH: He has every right to know if a person can add or perform the job at hand. But would he not want to know if a person can add to the atmosphere of a company or to the creativity of a task?

What would it hurt this employer to know these things? He would know more about his personnel and, therefore, more about his company.

FEAR: But if we don't grade, how are we going to distinguish one child from the next?
TRUTH: The answer is so obvious it's hardly worth articulating.

FEAR: Are you suggesting we describe each of our students, their strengths and weaknesses in each subject?
TRUTH: I'm suggesting we get to know our students. And they get to know themselves.

FEAR: That's not possible. There's no time.
TRUTH: Then there's no education.

FEAR: Of course there is—they're in school!
TRUTH: But they're not in touch.

FEAR: With what?
TRUTH: With themselves. With God.

FEAR: And what if a student does not believe in God?
TRUTH: It is of no matter. Believe then in your heart, in your own unique voice.

FEAR: It doesn't matter if a person believes in God?! The religious will have you hanged!
TRUTH: If people believe in their own heart, in their own unique voice, they still honor God. All is God.

FEAR: But they do not name the name.
TRUTH: Love is the Name.

FEAR: This is blasphemous according to many. For this, many feel you will go to hell.
TRUTH: Such judgment is already hell. Those who shut the door to heaven on others shut the door to heaven on themselves.

FEAR: And education also shuts this door, the door to heaven?
TRUTH: Where is the kingdom of heaven but within? It must come forth.

FEAR: The violinist must play his note?
TRUTH: All must play their note.

FEAR: And what note is this?
TRUTH: The note no one else can play—your own.

GENTLE CONTEMPT

✱

*When I was 5 years old, my mother always
told me that happiness was the key to life.
When I went to school, they asked me what
I wanted to be when I grew up. I wrote down
"happy." They told me I didn't understand the
assignment, and I told them they
didn't understand life.*

—JOHN LENNON

"WITHOUT A GENTLE CONTEMPT FOR EDUCATION no
gentleman's education is complete." This affable reproach by
G.K. Chesterton came to life in the fall of 2009, when my gentle
contempt for education surfaced as I delivered a convocation
address at Pepperdine University. Convocation is a required
faith-based gathering where students hear inspirational talks
from faculty, alumni, and professionals. After showing a few
clips from *Bruce Almighty; Liar, Liar;* and *Ace Ventura,* a student
asked how I felt about grades. It didn't take long to form an
answer: I'm less than a fan.

I started by letting out a curse word, calling grades, and I
quote, *"bullshit."* I doubled down on that curse word, saying the
SATs stood for Suck Ass Tests, and PSATs, Pretty Suck Ass. (Yes,
I have a bit of an attitude regarding aptitude tests!) I then told
the students the stress they feel over grades need not be; that it's
an illusion based on our adherence to the false god of hierarchy,

to the stratification of what cannot be stratified. Then, I told them the unthinkable: grades don't matter; what matters is the truth and doing their best. My rant went something like this:

If the truth is you do your best in math and you come up average, a mere C, then celebrate your ordinariness. If you score an A in history, then celebrate your excellence. Richard Branson admittedly can't read a spreadsheet and is doing just fine in the current paradigm. Einstein might have scored poorly if asked to write a Saturday Night Live *sketch, but if asked what scientific laws operate on Saturday night, would have surely impressed. Grades are of no consequence. Who you are is. Embrace your uniqueness, your strengths and weaknesses, your authenticity. And do not allow a sick system to tell you otherwise. God made the world and said that it was good. You are all part of that goodness.*

No sooner had I finished my remarks than the students leapt to their feet, breaking into wild applause. The ovation, I realized, was not for me; the students rose in unison for what they already knew: grades are grossly inadequate; they are a flat-out failure to articulate and differentiate our youths' particular talents, character, and complexities. Simply put, letter grades are utterly incapable of expressing the unique lights our students are.

But grades do not exist in a vacuum, nor do our schools. They are the outgrowth of a perspective gone awry, the reflection of who we are as a society and what we value: separation, stratification, winning. John Lennon is right; *we don't understand life.*

Case in point: many of our schools now teach to the test. And what kind of tests? Standardized. Money is awarded, teachers are promoted, schools are singled out when students meet limiting and arbitrary standards. But life does not standardize, nor does nature; so why should our schools? Nature abhors a standard, as do all who labor diligently and thoughtfully to create unique works of art. God is such an artist, creating countless life forms, no two of which are alike; no two trees, no two daisies, no two blades of grass. Are our kids not works of art as astonishing if not more so? How foolish to think we can accurately standardize such diversity? What does an SAT score tell you about a child's spirit, process, or imagination? Their ability to grow, listen, or adapt? These tests lay out inane problems, asking students to calculate the time of Jack and Janet's drive to the store. Better to imagine why Jack and Janet are headed to the store in the first place—for birth control, the munchies, maybe to buy a scratcher to pay off their exorbitant student loans, or to grab a Red Bull to stay up late studying for their lame standardized tests. Scoring poorly on the SAT is not an indicator of less intelligence. In certain cases, it just might be the opposite. Perhaps for some, we should call a low score what it is: a compliment.

Dialogue Twenty-one:

FEAR: You have an obvious ax to grind about standardized tests. Just because they didn't work for you doesn't mean they aren't good for others. For many, they are an accurate measurement of aptitude, intelligence, and ability.
TRUTH: They measure a certain kind of intelligence, yes.

FEAR: And you are upset because you don't have that kind of intelligence. Admit it, people who ace aptitude tests are smarter than you!

TRUTH: At aptitude tests, yes. But you, Fear, have long tried to turn me into what I am not. This fish is content with what he is and does not seek comparison with tree climbers.

FEAR: This is what you say, but you feel differently.

TRUTH: *You* feel differently. You tell people who they must become, so they do not recognize who they already are.

FEAR: So the problem is one of recognition?

TRUTH: Yes, recognition. To re-cognize. To rethink.

FEAR: To rethink what *I* tell them?

TRUTH: What society tells them, as well. It is not who they really are.

FEAR: Here's your chance: who are they?

TRUTH: The poet, Hafiz, said it best: *"God, disguised as myriad things and playing a game of tag has kissed you and said, 'You're it. I mean, you're really IT!'"*

FEAR: So we're all It?

TRUTH: Even you, Fear, play your part. For some, you are the beginning of wisdom. But only the beginning.

FEAR: And what happens to me after "the beginning"?
TRUTH: In the end, you will be seen for what your are—an illusion of the ego. And you will go the way of all illusions.

FEAR: And what way is that?
TRUTH: Perfect love will cast you out.

SCHADENFREUDE

✳

*Is it not the chief disgrace in the world . . .
not to yield that peculiar fruit which each man
was created to bear?*

—RALPH WALDO EMERSON

*Education is simply the soul of society
as it passes from one generation to the next.*

—G. K. CHESTERTON

THE FAMOUS HORSE WHISPERER Buck Brannaman touches upon a great truth when he says he does not help people with horse problems, but helps horses with people problems. Likewise, we are not a society with problematic schools; our schools come from a problematic society. How we teach and what we teach are not accidental; they are extensions of us—how we choose to live and what we live for, our obsession with winning, our dismissal of cooperation as utopian and unrealistic. We reach an inescapable conclusion: our schools are not the problem; *we are.*

A recent poll in the *Los Angeles Times* claims Californians are willing to pay higher taxes for better schools—but are we willing to pay the real price, which has little to do with money, and more to do with questioning what we value, what we teach, and who we have become? *"The least of the work of learning is done in classrooms,"* says Thomas Merton. He reminds us that learning extends to the shopping mall, the sporting event, the church hall, the daily commute, the ballot box, the grocery store, the social gathering, the dinner table. It is commonly accepted that teachers do the most important work in the world—but aren't we all teachers? Don't we all participate in our youths' unfolding, in the energy we call education? Whether you have children, are single or married, your behavior sends a message that emanates out and affects the whole. I have heard countless parents say they want their children to do whatever makes them happy. Yet those same parents do not do what makes them happy. Their words fall on deaf ears. *"I can't hear what you're saying over all that you're doing,"* is the child's right response. *"You want me to follow my bliss, yet you don't follow yours?"* All is education. All is preaching. A teacher teaches at the chalkboard; the rest of us teach with our lives. There is no escaping it. Even if you disdain preaching, you still preach a message about your disdain for preaching! Better to accept the reality: the oak tree instructs; the sunset delivers a daily sermon. The question isn't *"Are* you preaching?" but *"What* are you preaching?" Are you preaching the old story of competition and winning, the tired German school of schadenfreude, *"I will never be truly successful until I see all my friends fail"*? Or are you preaching the coming revolution? Are you doing your part, not small but essential, to birth a new way of being and walking in this world? Yes, we should salute the instructor in the classroom, but also in the boardroom, the lunchroom, and living room. *"Preach the gospel wherever you can; when all else fails use words."* St. Francis's edict is a divine imperative. His admonition begs a different question—not *"How do we fix education?"* but *"How do we fix ourselves?"*

✳

REMEMBER THE CONVOCATION where I spoke up about grades? It was recorded, like all convocations, but when several students requested a copy of the talk, they were told the tape had somehow been "lost." To this day, it remains the only convocation tape ever "misplaced" in the history of Pepperdine. I consider it high praise, a nudge from the ether that my gentle contempt for education is alive and well, and happily so. For all is dependent upon education: our happiness is dependent on the lesson plan in the classroom; our economy is just one way education plays out. We must do better. No student is a standard but a story unfolding. And learning, in the truest sense, is not a pouring in of new facts, but a pulling out of the Ancient Fact. Let education, then, be a key, and no more; a key to the doorway of the human heart, a key to unlock what has been inside us all along: the Infinite Cause, the Divine Spark, the Kingdom of Heaven Itself.

Dialogue Twenty-two:

FEAR: You stand alone in your criticism of education. Even the President of the United States is on my side.
TRUTH: Even presidents can be fearful.

FEAR: Let the reader decide. Here is his letter on the Department of Education's Website:

Every child in America deserves a world-class education.

Today, more than ever, a world-class education is a prerequisite for success. America was once the best educated nation in the world. A generation ago, we led all nations in college completion, but today, 10 countries have passed us. It is not that their students are smarter than ours. It is that these countries are being smarter about how to educate their students. And the countries that out-educate us today will out-compete us tomorrow.

We must do better. Together, we must achieve a new goal, that by 2020, the United States will once again lead the world in college completion. We must raise the expectations for our students, for our schools, and for ourselves—this must be a national priority. We must ensure that every student graduates from high school well prepared for college and a career.

Sincerely,
Barack Obama
President of the United States

TRUTH: Since you have offered our President's point of view, let me respectfully, offer my own:

Dear Mr. President,

I couldn't agree more; every child does deserve a world-class education. But certainly we will differ on what is meant by a "world-class education." Your letter seems to define it singularly as the completion of college; that this is a prerequisite for success.

College is a prerequisite for success? Should I bother to name the thousands, if not millions of people who did not go to college who turned out okay in the scheme of things; people who may have been homeschooled or mentored, or were educated by life itself and its many challenges? Jim Carrey, one of the greatest artists of our generation, never finished high school. Einstein struggled mightily in academia. Do you realize, Mr. President, that many of the signers of our Constitution did not have what we would call a traditional education—that many were schooled through apprenticeships?

"Ah," but some will say, "they were not of today's world." And what makes today's world so different? Do not the same things lead to lives of meaning, purpose, and contentment? Did we not yesterday, as today, take the deepest joy in loving our fellow man, in appreciating the gift of life, in edifying the soul and spirit, in serving the greater good? And how is it you categorically state we were once the best educated nation on earth? How do you know? Your definition of "best educated" is remarkably narrow; here you only include the numerical tally of those graduating from college. What do these numbers really tell us about how "educated" a person is? Isn't it possible a person might have book knowledge yet little wisdom? If these numbers are so important, why do Americans have the highest recorded rates of drug abuse and addiction, and the second-highest rate of depression in the world? And what about other cultures where the approach to education differs, but whose citizens are healthy and content? Are the Kogi Indians, who know how to respect and care for the earth, less educated? What about the Tibetan masters? They lacked "college" as an institution in the traditional sense. Is not their understanding of life and its values— of art and drama, their appreciation of virtue and the soul—not what you would term "best educated"?

The author of this very book attended a highly respected college, the University of Virginia, was Phi Beta Kappa, and frankly, doesn't remember a thing he studied. He has, however, for the past 25 years, without the pressure or directives of any authority, passionately pursued learning—listening to his heart, honoring his love of poetry, philosophy, spirituality, and storytelling. In the arts, he has spent years with Stella Adler, Sanford Meisner, Lee Strasberg, and Uta Hagen. He has read—no, consumed!—Emerson, Lao Tzu, Rilke, Rumi, and Hafiz. None of this was required, no papers to turn in, no reports to be graded. Did learning not take place? Was he not educated in this process? And no, it was not college that prepared him for these studies. College did the opposite—discouraging him from any pursuit where a dollar sign was not the obvious outcome, where a job did not lay waiting.

Mr. President, can we not at least note that we've only been schooling ourselves within the narrow confines of our current definition for a small percentage of human history? Must we ignore the wisdom and knowledge of 170,000 years of our species' experience? The aborigines did not read books, but could read the stars. Were they not educated? Why do we insist on applying such a limited and linear definition to learning; is it not a color that comes in many shades?

And now comes the real poison of your argument: that countries that out-educate us today will out-compete us tomorrow. May I risk the label of heretic and say, "So what?" So what if we are number two or number five? Won't the sun still rise and the moon come up? Why are we so obsessed with being number one? If we are to be obsessed with something, why not be obsessed with the truth? And if the truth is, after giving it our all, we are third in math, or second in science, is that so tragic? Perhaps we will show the highest levels of creativity and caring for each other; perhaps we will be the envy of the world when it comes to the peace and love evident in our hearts. Don't you consider yourself a Christian, Mr. President? If being number one is so important, why did the greatest moral teacher in history leave it out of his doctrine? If you recall, he said the meek will inherit the earth, not the gold medalists.

Being number one has little to do with the pursuit of excellence, which is a pursuit worthy of our nation's time and attention. We all would be well advised to do the best we can, to serve our passions and talents with all we are—but the numerical result is unimportant, and an unnecessary drain on our emotions and our focus. The great basketball coach, John Wooden, felt the same. Winning, he said, was of little concern. There were many games he felt his team lost even though they came out ahead, and many they won, even though they came up short. Winning is giving one's full effort, and facing a challenge with courage and dedication; it is not a statistic on a score sheet.

Lastly, you state education must be a national priority. Here we agree—but can we at least have a national dialogue about what it means to be educated? Consider that the original definition of the term is its most potent: to draw out the light and talents of the individual—as Emerson said, to set the soul aflame. This may just be how God walks in the world—using our hands and feet, experiencing life through our passions and purpose. If the kingdom of heaven is indeed within, as Jesus said, then what we call forth is not insignificant; perhaps it is the will of God Itself.

Sincerely,
Tom Shadyac's Truth

FEAR: Your letter is disrespectful. And you have little authority in this area.

TRUTH: Nature is the authority. And as she demonstrates, a species that idealizes competition and winning cannot sustain itself.

FEAR: And what do you want in place of winning? You want education to be fun!

TRUTH: And why can't it be fun? Why can't we allow children extended time to play, to create, to walk in nature? These behaviors are in perfect sync with how humans learn.

FEAR: Children learn through play? They learn to waste time, that's what they learn. Learning isn't supposed to be fun. It's meant to be difficult.

TRUTH: Is it? How difficult is it for a child to first learn a language? To first learn to explore an object of interest? The child is equipped with curiosity, curiosity leads to experience, and experience teaches the child. Undue effort is required only when we force children to learn what they are not ready to learn, what they do not wish to learn. Ultimately then, what we create is not learning, but unhappiness in our students, and unhappiness within our school system.

FEAR: Happiness has no place in this conversation.

TRUTH: Happiness *is* the conversation.

FEAR: We're talking about education!

TRUTH: And what is the goal of education if not to produce a happy citizenry?

FEAR: It's to produce a *successful* citizenry. Successful people do not waste their time talking about fluff. Happiness is a sentiment. It's of no practical value.

TRUTH: Then you do not understand happiness. Happiness is rooted in practicality. What is happiness, essentially, but an indication that a system is working well? An engine that runs smoothly, or a computer that operates efficiently—each is said to be happy, is it not? And is it not the same with a human life? If the economy is working well, if education is doing its job, would abounding happiness not be the inevitable result? This is the subject of our final exploration—what is this condition we call happiness? And how can each of us, swimming in a sea of social pressure, find or be found by the Declaration of Independence's most hallowed pursuit?

HAPPINESS

✳

When all your desires are distilled,
You will cast just two votes:
To love more,
And be happy.

—HAFIZ

THIS WRITING, I TRUST, will not be your typical essay on happiness; too many have taken on the subject and written the conventions before—*watch a sunrise, spend more time with your family, exercise, slow down, do something good for someone else, adopt a puppy.* Google the subject and you'll be hit with a thousand treatises, each claiming to identify the six steps to help you experience this sacred state. Quite frankly, the six steps bore me; not to diminish their power—they are, indeed, helpful and true—but the interest here is not to simply identify steps; the interest here is to foster a dialogue about the dynamics of happiness—why these six steps (or seven or eight) work in the first place. What principles are they resting on, and what do these principles reveal about who we are and what makes us thrive as individuals, as a species?

First, a confession: I'm not a fan of the word—certainly not how it's been popularized in today's culture. *Happiness.* It's misleading. Even the field that has developed to study its laws, Positive Psychology, chose a one-sided label. *Positive.* To talk about happiness in its truest sense is not to focus only on the positive. And that's where these glossy labels have let us down. They imply favorable circumstances. The word *happiness* itself originally meant good luck, fortune, and prosperity. It suggests that the world is best viewed through rose-colored glasses. I for one like my glasses clear. I don't want my landscapes colored in rose. I want my shadows deep, my blacks, black. To talk only about positivity is to take one side of a two-sided coin. Light is always accompanied by shadow; the highest tide here means the lowest ebb there. Polarity exits and cannot be gotten rid of; every up has its down, every north, its south. As Emerson says: *"We can no more halve things and get the sensual good, by itself, than we can get an inside that shall have no outside."*

And so it is with happiness—it must be viewed more holistically; a tear and a smile. True happiness does not refer to some Pollyanna state of bliss with chirping birds and floating butterflies; it does not imply a person walking on air 24/7. We've all seen them, synthetic smiles frozen in place, too many teeth exposed, in deadened denial even as the world is falling apart. That's not happy, that's creepy. True contentment—*contentment* might be a truer term, as it's rooted in content, what's on the inside—allows and even welcomes the comings and goings of good fortune and favor. A negative event, a disease, a deprivation, a loss, may in fact, prove the best of luck. My concussion and facing my own death was a perfect and precise blessing. We are told to think positively. Is it not wiser to think truthfully? When the mystic Julian of Norwich said, *"All shall be well, and all shall be well, and all manner of thing shall be well,"* she used the verb *shall,* not *is;* and in this, the temporal, there are difficulties that exist, sorrows that arise, mutilations that affect. If you've recently lost a son or daughter in the war, or are struggling with addiction, all is not presently well. But a deeper consideration reveals the inalterable truth: that out of these deaths come new life; that difficulties and deprivation are the ashes from which new epochs arise; and given time, that perfect healer, even dark days begin to glow with the light of purpose.

The Sufis point the way when they define their own religion as *"the feeling of joy when sudden disappointment comes."* How much faith must a Sufi possess to experience true joy at sudden disappointment! And why joy? Because of the unshakeable trust that something is being born, that the dead skin of an old habit is falling away. And this is what truly happy people know: sorrow and sadness, disappointment and loss, are part of life; trials and tribulations are difficult but necessary guides. With a deep faith that abides in the knowledge that everything that happens, the Great Teacher staged, they are able to see challenges for what they are: corrections, the refiner's fire.

In a scene that was cut from *Bruce Almighty,* God gives Bruce a glimpse into how things really work. For those who haven't seen the film, Bruce was given God's power to answer prayer, and out of laziness and sheer ignorance, Bruce says yes to every request. In one instance, he grants a boy being bullied the strength to beat up his tormentors. Bruce, of course, does not foresee the connected chain of events set in motion by his affirmative response. He does not see that this boy's authentic calling was to turn his pain into poetry; his art would one day move millions. Instead, thanks to Bruce's table-turning intervention, the boy is now on his way to becoming a wrestler on cable TV—a fine occupation if that is your true calling, but it was not true for this boy. And so, referring to the potential beauty of this future poet, God articulates a truth we too often wish to ignore: *"To paint a picture like this, you've got to use some dark colors."* And that's the point really, that as a society, as individuals, we have not yet learned to embrace our dark colors; we only wish to paint in pastels. It's why the poet Rumi (who I'm guessing was not granted the strength to beat up his tormentors!) states this truth: *"The rose celebrates by falling apart . . . the cloud celebrates by weeping."*

This deep and destructive addiction of our culture, the desire to escape difficulties, the wish to avoid all pain, is why so many people lead quiet lives of desperation. Trials hone, and without that honing, our edges dull. We drink and take drugs to numb out; we watch TV to tune out; the sad fact is that we would rather be distracted than disturbed. But we have it upside down; when we are disturbed, we have a chance to learn something. Happy people, content people, know this and accept the instructive force the pain of separation and loss has to offer. This is the theme of M. Scott Peck's masterwork, *The Road Less Traveled*—the road is *less* traveled precisely because it is difficult. But truth cannot be gotten around: To avoid pain in the present ensures that it will be suffered in the future, pressed down and shaken together. There is no escaping the consequences of a life half-lived. Avoid a difficult talk with a lover, spouse, or friend; ignore your true calling for comfort and safety; evade a duty—and the ensuing ease will prove short-lived. Truth suppressed festers. But pain seen in the light of perspective reveals itself as a gift. It is pressure, and only pressure, that turns the lump of coal into a diamond. Even the green army recruit knows to shout with all he has, *"Thank you sir, may I have another?!"*

The gospel of the positive is half a gospel. I recently attended a popular seminar that proclaims to its participants, *"Yes you can!"* But I say, from time to time, *"Perhaps, you can't!"* And that's a good thing, because in limitation, in loss, comes perspective, guidance, appreciation. Frankly, I am tired of people writing books entitled *Ageless Body, Timeless Mind* while getting old in front of us. I don't mean to rain on *The Secret's* parade, but our thoughts don't create reality. God creates reality. Our thoughts profoundly affect how we experience that reality. You can entertain every positive thought possible, but if you're 5′1″, you're not going to think your way to 7 feet and play in the NBA. If you were born into the famines of Ethiopia, no thought is going to save you; food will. I know this puts a damper on many of those vision boards—I often wonder how Jesus lived without one—but what is it we are envisioning for ourselves if not the will of God? If heaven has a newspaper, vision boards must be in the comics section, for the only way to make God laugh harder than telling Him your plans, is to show Him your vision board. Every time I thought I knew what was best for me, God had a better idea. I wanted to direct a short-lived sitcom called *She's the Sheriff;* God wanted me to direct *Ace Ventura.* I wanted to continue making blockbuster commercial movies; God hit me over the head and wanted me to share my story in *I AM.* And by God—I repeat myself, but it bears repeating—I am not referring to any force outside of ourselves. We are It, the hands and feet of Divinity. If God is omnipresent, then He exists in every part and particle, and certainly in you and me.

Wet cannot be separated from water. But ego has indeed, edged god out, and poisons our connection with our Highest Self, and hence, God. That's why, in *Bruce Almighty,* when Bruce tells God he wants more money, a better apartment, and a better job, God hits Bruce with a haymaker of truth: *"Since when does anyone have a clue about what they want?"*

Lastly, with all due respect to our nation's Declaration of Independence, I submit that when it comes to happiness, Thomas Jefferson was wrong. Happiness is not a pursuit, it's a practice. In *Zen in the Art of Archery,* the Zen archer possesses such accuracy, he is not only able to hit a bull's-eye, he is able to split the arrow in the bull's-eye with another arrow. And here we confront the paradox: the archer splits the arrow by *not* trying to split the arrow. He focuses on process only, on the position of the bow, the grip of the arrow, the drawing back of the bowstring. His concentration is so deep, the archer and the target are no longer two separate objects. And thus, without thought, without a result in mind, the shot looses itself and the arrow is split. It is the goalless goal. As the Chinese master Chuang Tzu said, *"When an archer is shooting for nothing, he has all his skill."*

So it is I believe, with happiness. We don't become happy by focusing on happiness, by pursuing it; we focus instead on what is true, what is good, what is right—and happiness follows. Is it right and good that we spend more time with our families, that we devote ourselves to a higher purpose, that we express ourselves authentically, uniquely, truthfully? Then do so, and the happiness arrow will be split. I did not change my life with the conscious intention of becoming happier, and yet I did become happier, immeasurably so. I made choices and acted in each instance, because these actions felt good and right. I did not give more money away to be happier; I gave money away because it felt like the right thing to do. I did not move into the mobile home park to become happier; I moved there because living a simpler life felt like the right thing to do. With each step into the good and right, happiness was the inevitable result. I had stumbled upon a principle Aristotle had articulated 2,000 years ago: *Virtue and happiness are one and the same.*

In retrospect, my life reads like a happiness case study: a happy child is co-opted by a vision of the world that values the illusory; as a young professional, he struggles for contentment; over time, he is awakened to certain principles and then finds peace and joy. The parable may prove instructive, as many are still lost in the deception, unaware. So let's take a look back to see just what poison I swallowed, and just what antidote brought relief. How exactly did I become happier? And what principles reveal themselves that can help you, too, become like C.S. Lewis himself—*Surprised by Joy?*

Dialogue Twenty-three:

FEAR: So much of what you say goes against conventional wisdom. That we should be glad when we are unsettled. That comfort is not what we should aspire to. It's only wise to take care of ourselves, to seek security. When you're on an airplane, you put on your oxygen mask first!
TRUTH: Not when the person beside you is dying and you have breath to spare. Too many today are dying and far too many have breath to spare.

FEAR: But people want to be comfortable. What's wrong with that? I don't see what's wrong with not wanting to be in pain.
TRUTH: Look at the word *comfort*. It is a combination of two words: *come*, meaning to welcome, and *fort*, which is a structure built to shut out all danger, all risk. To live, to really live, one must embrace risk; one must tear down these walls and invite in all of life.

FEAR: So you would have us be uncomfortable for our entire lives? Who wants to live like that?!
TRUTH: I would have you find comfort in the discomfort. You say it is only natural and right to want to avoid pain. It is also natural and right to want to grow, and pain is growth's prerequisite. Do you not see that from your pain, your passions spring forth? The black minister born into the segregated south who dedicates his life to justice for all; the rehabilitated alcoholic who now counsels those still bound by addiction. Life exists in the belly of a paradox, and the paradox is this: pain is found inside of beauty, and beauty inside of pain. As the wisdom teaching instructs, *"Shield the mountain from the winds and you will miss the beauty of the carvings."*

FEAR: And I say get out of the wind! Wind destroys. Wind can kill! This is why people use vision boards, to create a better life, to avoid all of this pain. And this is why you object to them!
TRUTH: I have no objection to vision boards. It simply depends on how a vision board is used.

FEAR: Like all vision boards, you put up a picture of something you want, and hopefully, you get it!

TRUTH: If a vision board is used to bring forth the truth that is in you, a vision board is a tool for good. If a vision board is used to get something for ego's sake, why not trade it for a gun? Both are tools for robbery. As Emerson has warned us, *"The highest price [a man] can pay for a thing is to ask for it."*

FEAR: So now it's wrong to ask for things? Doesn't your good book say *"ask and it shall be given to you"*?

TRUTH: Asking for a thing is not what is important. What is important is *why* we are asking for a thing. Do you want something that originates in your own heart, in the desire to bring forth God's will? Or has society placed the desire there, molding you into a product of its making?

FEAR: But don't most of you dreamers believe we can have whatever we want by changing our thoughts? Jesus fed the masses fishes and loaves with just a thought. Can't we do the same?

TRUTH: So you think we can end hunger with a thought, with intention?

FEAR: Many dreamers do, yes. They say we can manifest whatever we put our minds to.

TRUTH: Then why end at fishes and loaves? Why not, with our thoughts and intentions, manifest houses and end homelessness? And while we're at it, why not, with our thoughts, manifest cleanliness and eliminate the need to sweep and mop floors? Why not manifest food, clean water, shelter, and medicine for all, and do away with our need to serve each other? Is this not the logical end of the power of our thoughts, of manifestation? If we can think everything up, why do we even have hands and feet? Why would God even want us or need us?

FEAR: God needs us?
TRUTH: How else can the Creator experience His creation, if not through our eyes, if not through our feet? Thoughts are a start, always. But thoughts must translate into action. Thoughts must compel us to walk in the world—not away from difficulty, but toward it.

FEAR: All of this talk of difficulty, of pain. The story you are selling is so negative. It is hard for people to accept.
TRUTH: When will you understand, Fear, that all compelling stories involve difficulty. And the greater the difficulty that is overcome, the greater the story. It is not an accident that shit makes the best fertilizer. Why not embrace it? When you are standing in it up to your metaphorical knees, why not grow a garden?

SHOW ME THE MONEY!

✳

To be clever enough to get all that money,
one must be stupid enough to want it.

—G.K. CHESTERTON

A great fortune is a great slavery.

—SENECA

EVERY WEEKEND IN LOS ANGELES, AM radio gives itself over to infomercials, and every week, I hear a talk show that is representative of what I term *our collective insanity*. This weekly infomercial promises to make you rich, to make your life stress-free, and to welcome you into the ranks of the well-to-do. Just learn the wealth-generating principles in the presenting author's book, and you, too, can lead the good life; you, too, can be happy. But what if the advertisement for this money-making program went something like this:

I guarantee to make you a millionaire in six months or less! That's right, because I'm the millionaire maker! And when you buy my book and follow my system, sure, you'll have more money, but in all probability, you won't be any happier than you are right now! And with all the complications of this newfound wealth, you might just be less happy! And you know that hole you feel inside? The money won't fill that either! So what are you waiting for—get my system and get less happy today!

Now that sounds crazy, right? No one would want that book or take that bait. And yet, all of the happiness research to date suggests that this is exactly the case—*that money, after it purchases basic needs, does not make people any happier and can, in fact, make us less happy.* How is it then, that those who have made money, and tons of it, the newest members of the jet set and Fortune 500, are often elevated and honored—monopolizing the headlines to share secrets of how they did it, and how we can do it, too? There are *Billionaires Under 50, Millionaires Under 25,* and *Teenage Self-made Millionaires!* Undoubtedly, *Affluent Adolescents* and *Baby Billionaires* are just around the corner! But with all we know now about the failings of money to deliver a happy and contented citizenry, we somehow still seem to be missing the message. After all, if money is such a panacea, why is the richest country on earth experiencing record levels of anxiety, depression, and suicide? Why then do we continue to teach our children that the good life is preceded and underscored by a dollar sign? If you don't believe we're teaching this to our kids, consider this startling statistic: 74 percent of our youth identify economic gain as the primary reason to go to college; not the pursuit of one's passion, not for edification; not for relationships or the mind's expansion. Our youth enter our hallowed institutions demanding not that their souls be set aflame, but bellowing that fateful line from *Jerry Maguire,* "*Show me the money!*"

Somewhere, there's a disconnection; somehow, we continue to ignore the simple fact that wealth and well-being have little to do with each other. Case in point: After a screening of *I AM* at a local college here in Southern California, a student rose up, tilted his head to the side and asked a question in utter confusion: *"You're telling me you left a mansion to live in a trailer park?"* I confirmed that indeed I had, but then delivered the kicker—I told him I had become happier in the process. Confusion quickly digressed to disbelief, his expression resembling that of the stupefied RCA dog. *"Who would leave an MTV crib for a trailer?"* Ah, yes, *MTV Cribs,* that most egregious show that equates artistic success with material excess, painting a picture for kids of the unsustainable—and for most, the unattainable. All this from a *music* network— music, an art form steeped in the pursuit of a more equitable, just, and loving world, now unashamedly selling itself out to the very conformity it historically rebels against. But back to our confused student, who simply could not comprehend how downsizing in square footage could lead to upsizing in well-being. I further explained that although I had traded a mansion for a double-wide, I had somehow walked into the principles that produce a happy life: *simplicity*—17,000 square feet had become 1,000; *community*—neighbors, walled out in the past by electric gates and six-foot fences, became friends; and *authenticity*—a castle in the suburbs was my society's vision, a cabin by the sea was my own.

Sadly, this elucidation did little to ease the perplexity of this stunned student. And herein lies the challenge: When it comes to happiness, our society has taught us that up is down, and down is up. Our stuck student has been so primed by his culture to believe that bigger is better, my experience to the contrary could not convince him otherwise. And this is really the issue. How do we arouse and reorient a citizenry lulled to sleep by society's hypnotic messaging, which focuses our attention on the treasure that moth and rust destroy, instead of on the kingdom within?

✻

THERE WAS A famous study in the early 1990s in which the subjects were told to count the number of times a basketball was passed back and forth by the "red" team versus the number of passes executed by the "yellow" team. During the basketball game, a man in a gorilla suit walks right across the court, and get this, virtually no one notices. That's a man in a gorilla suit, not a man in khakis or camouflage. But the subjects are so busy counting passes, a six-foot man wrapped in rubber and fur passes them by without their conscious awareness. And is it not accurate to say the same of us? That our culture keeps us so busy counting money and material possessions, focusing our attention on status symbols and skewed definitions of success, that our own happiness, anchored in family, community, creativity, simplicity and service—is passing us by with little to no recognition?

This is certainly what happened in my adult life. I was told happiness was *out there,* in the counting. And happiness, of course, passed me by. And yet, as a child, I was profoundly happy, to the point where I walked with a blissful, literal, skip in my step. Call it naïveté (I prefer purity), there was no such thing as a routine stroll, only another opportunity to glide in celebration over a hill, down a dirt path, along a stream. As Mary Oliver says, *"fields everywhere invite you into them,"* and I knew no better (there is no better!) than to excitedly accept their invitation.

What is it the child knows about happiness, passion, and play, that the adult forgets? Eastern philosophers believe we are all born with a connection to, and knowledge of, the essential elements for happiness. Thus, in the poem "Keng's Disciple," Chuang Tzu issues the following instructions to a student struggling with his own contentment:

> *You want the first elements?*
> *The infant has them.*
> *Free from care, unaware of self,*
> *He acts without reflection,*
> *Stays where he is put, does not know why,*
> *Does not figure things out,*
> *Just goes along with them,*
> *Is part of the current.*
> *These are the first elements!*

Judeo-Christian doctrine echoes Chuang Tzu's sentiment: *"Unless ye become like these little children, ye shall not enter the kingdom of heaven."* If Jesus's admonition is true, that children are indeed closer to the kingdom, is it not worth asking why? Why is it, exactly, that Henry David Thoreau always regretted the fact that he was not as wise as the day he was born?

Dialogue Twenty-four:

FEAR: Why do you insist on putting children on a pedestal? Doesn't your scripture say that when you became a man you put away childish things?

TRUTH: The same scripture says, *"Thank you, Father, for hiding these things from the wise and learned and revealing them to little children."*

FEAR: But Chuang Tzu's words are irresponsible. To admire a child who has no care? To admire a child because he does not reflect? What kind of society would we have if people were free from care?
TRUTH: Perhaps a healthier one.

FEAR: A lazier one! If people were free from care nothing would get done. The reason people get things done is they are not free from care. They care!
TRUTH: Are you aware that two synonyms for care are *worry* and *concern?* Worry is not the natural state of the child. It is taught to him by a fearful society. It is taught to him by you.

FEAR: I protect the child! From danger! From suffering!
TRUTH: From life. Do you not see that suffering is a part of life and will always remain so? Worry will not alter the fact.

FEAR: If worry is not the natural state of the child, what is?
TRUTH: According to Lao Tzu, it is love. Pure love.

FEAR: And what is my natural state? I know what you will say—it is worry!
TRUTH: And now you will worry that you worry.

FEAR: Ahh! It is all so confusing!
TRUTH: It does not have to be.

FEAR: What would you have me do?
TRUTH: Relax your grip.

FEAR: I will sink.
TRUTH: You will float.

FEAR: And what will hold me up?
TRUTH: The same force that holds the planets in rotation, that moves the blood in the veins.

FEAR: This is what the child knows?
TRUTH: This is what the child is.

LITTLE TOMMY SHADYAC

✳

With much ado I was corrupted,
and made to learn the dirty devices of this world,
which now I unlearn, and become, as it were,
a little child again that I may
enter into the kingdom of God.

—THOMAS TRAHERNE

THE MOST UNLIKELY, unremarkable event changed the course of my life. It was not a parting of the clouds, an angelic choir, or a heavenly trumpet roar that did it; it was not a tragic turn or a sobering diagnosis. The event that changed my life and set a course of other events into motion is almost too simple to mention. I bought a bike. *"How's that, you say? You didn't have a nervous breakdown? There was no intervention? The cops didn't throw you in morality jail?"* No. I'll say it again, because on the surface, it really is quite underwhelming. The end result though, was anything but: I bought a bicycle.

It's quite indicative that our brow furrows at the mention of such a tiny act. You see, most of us greatly underestimate *the power of changing one simple thing in our lives.* One small shift, one reworking of a behavior or habit, sends out a ripple of energy and, when seen in the light and context of time, moves mountains. Bob Zemeckis's iconic time-travel movie *Back to the Future* is a perfect illustration. By stepping into a doctored DeLorean, Marty McFly (Michael J. Fox) travels back 30 years to 1955, and quickly realizes that changing anything in the past, even the smallest action, will radically alter the future. One kindness extended, one cruelty carried out, a meeting interfered with, and decades later, the future is forever redirected. That's the power of a single act—the infinite reach of the butterfly effect—to alter, shift, and shape reality. It's physics, really. Try it for yourself: bounce a tennis ball off a wall, and the ball will bounce back the same way every time; now change the angle of that wall one degree, just one degree, and the ball will never bounce back the same way again. In my life, buying a bike changed the wall one degree. Here's how:

Show business might as well be called Slow Business, as it takes a long time and lots of man-hours to make a movie. The average eight-hour workday is unheard of—eight hours on a movie set isn't a workday, it's a holiday. A film director's duties generally begin before sunup and go well past sunset. Over the course of my career, it was not unusual to work 16 to 18 hours a day, six days a week, for months on end. There was little time for rest, to walk in nature, to breathe. After 14 years of filmmaking, life had spun woefully out of balance and I knew enough, just enough, to do something about it.

As simple as it seems, the decision to buy a bike was, in itself, a small act of rebellion; it was a subtle rejection of the live-to-work versus the work-to-live mentality I had grown so accustomed to and weary of. It was step one in a conscious reordering of priorities. And the priority of our culture is made painfully clear the day our schooling begins; we are to stop horsing around and get serious with our lives. Buying this bike flipped the messaging on its head—it was time to get serious, alright; it was time to get serious about horsing around. The mystic Thomas Merton was in full agreement when he said:

What is serious to men is often very trivial in the sight of God. What in God, might appear to us as "play" is perhaps what He himself takes most seriously.

And so, in the fall of 2002, I entered a sporting goods store in the foothills of Pasadena with one simple thought: it's time to play again. I made my way to the bike rack, picked out one of those two-wheeled wonders, and took it for a test ride in the parking lot—not even sure how to switch gears, how high to set the seat, or what lever engaged which brake. But weaving figure eights on smooth, dark asphalt stirred a familiar but long-forgotten sensation, flashes of the buoyancy of youth resurfaced, and my body, my whole being, screamed, *"Yes!"*

World-renowned environmental activist John Francis knows what I'm referring to. After witnessing an oil spill in 1972, John gave up all motorized transportation and walked for 22 years, 17 of those years in silence. When I interviewed John for *I AM,* I asked him what he discovered after all of that listening. *"Little Johnny Francis,"* he said. Two decades of solitude and silence were summed up in one startlingly simple realization: *the authenticity of his childhood, the joy, the sense of wonder, the purity, had been reborn.* In his autobiography, *Planetwalker,* John recalls growing up in the 1960s amid severe societal pressures and becoming co-opted into a vision of the world that was not his own. As a child, he came alive in nature, on long walks, strolls on the beach, in the woods. But as he grew up, he was told what success looked like: it wears a coat and a tie, and it walks as a doctor, a lawyer, or an entrepreneur. It was not until he left the clamor of society, the voices telling him how to be and who to be, that his own true voice emerged. It turns out, John was not a doctor, or a lawyer; John Francis was a walker, a lover of nature, an advocate.

I, too, have walked into silence before, and felt the profound effects of deep listening. In 1996, the day after the opening of *Liar, Liar,* I traded the media madness of our movie's release for the temporary solitude of Gethsemani, Thomas Merton's Trappist monastery in the tranquil hills of Kentucky. I brought nothing to the retreat—no reading material, no phone, no computer—just a journal to record my thoughts and a willingness to be led by the experience. And lead me it did— into the unexpected, unanticipated joys of my youth. Without forethought or premeditation, I began to walk again as a child— no, not walk, *skip*! I hopped from stone to stone along a riverbed and marveled at the life bursting around me: wildflowers, tall grasses, turtles, and water bugs. I counted rings in tree stumps; I whittled. Of all things, I whittled! I had not whittled since summer camp, 1967; I was nine years old then, and here I was, doing it again, naturally, spontaneously, joyfully. The silence engulfed me; I became as the mystics have promised, empty but full; and a new voice emerged, a truer voice: *my own.* What Wordsworth's *Prelude* lamented I could no longer see, I saw; all of creation was once again *"apparell'd in celestial light."*

I returned to the city determined to retain the perspective that had infused my monastic experience. Try as I might, the child in me fell silent, his light buried under an avalanche of expectations. I was no longer a human being, but a human doing. It would take years for that still, small voice to speak again; it would take the odd purchase of that bike.

I rode to the grocery store, into the mountains, to the beach, to work. And with each pedal stroke, like a turbine harnessing the wind's power, the child in me got stronger. I doubled down on this sense of play, waxed up a surfboard and caught a wave for the first time in two decades. Again the child leapt, instantly reawakened to the euphoric energy that is surfing. The culture hissed: *"People who are serious about making it do not waste their time riding bikes!" "They are called surf bums for a reason!"* The child shot back: *"What you call wasting time, I call church."*

This push and pull went on, a struggle for control between the head and the heart, between the two wolves that live inside. By taking time to bike, surf, and walk in nature, I fed the wolf of my truth and strode further into authenticity. Changes came quickly. When I woke up to mankind's abuse of the natural world and my participation in that abuse, I stopped flying privately, a perk frequently granted to the show-business elite. The fearful wolf lashed out:

FEAR: Are you crazy? You can fly anywhere, anytime you want!
TRUTH: We live in a limited world, and I am using more than my share of resources.

FEAR: It's called an inconvenient truth for a reason!
TRUTH: No truth, in the end, is inconvenient.

When I sold the Pasadena estate and moved into a mobile home park, Fear continued its attack:

FEAR: It's a double-wide, for godsakes!
TRUTH: It's all I need.

FEAR: You don't even own the land!
TRUTH: Ownership is an illusion.

FEAR: You have to own things!
TRUTH: I own this choice.

And when I decided to give more money away, retooling the way I approached economy in my life, Fear couldn't take it:

FEAR: What about your future? You'll starve!
TRUTH: Others are starving now.

FEAR: Years from now you might need that money! What if you get sick? You could die!
TRUTH: If I don't do what's right today, I'm dead already.

FEAR: What do you want to do, give away all your money?!
TRUTH: It was never ours in the first place.

FEAR: If you're not a millionaire, if you walk away from all this, what will you be?!
TRUTH: What I've always been. Myself.

Fear might have fared better if it weren't for one irrefutable fact: the changes in my life—embracing play, community, simplicity, and sharing—brought untold feelings of peace and joy. This shook Fear to the core:

FEAR: How could this be? Everything we're doing is the opposite of what we've been told.
TRUTH: And we've stumbled into the opposite feeling: *happiness.*

FEAR: But money, power, prestige—they should make us happy! Things should make us happy!

(Truth placed a reassuring hand on Fear's shoulder.)

TRUTH: There you go again, Fear, always "shoulding" on yourself.

Fear, of course, has never gone away completely, but his bark no longer has bite. He's like a dog that snarls out of anxiety: face it and it whimpers away, tail between its legs. In the end, what Fear really can't stand is someone, anyone, you or me, who dares to be oneself. Jesus said, *unless you leave mother, father, sister and brother, you are not worthy of me.* This is not a literal commandment to leave your family, but a metaphorical one. Unless you can reject the dreams of others—of mother, father, sister, and brother—you will never find your own; you will never live an authentic life.

The plain fact is, happiness and authenticity have everything to do with each other. We all walk this earth, utterly unique expressions of the Divine, with particular talents and perspectives that need to be brought forth. And if they are not brought forth, not only does our happiness suffer, our soul's light, the light that we are here to express, fades. We all know people dying a little each day because they are not following their hearts. If you are working for money, prestige, or power, or to please the expectations of others in defiance of the truth that is in you, you will pay the ultimate price, for you have turned age-old wisdom inside out; you have gained your life, and therefore, you will lose it.

Here's the question: what is fear keeping you from saying, doing, exploring, being? It's a question we must face if we are to move from boredom to bliss, from bondage to freedom. It cannot be answered with words alone; it requires action, stepping willfully, directly, boldly out of our comfort zone and into the unknown—*"the dark forest,"* as Joseph Campbell called it. This is the hero's journey: to face your fear; to see it for the paper tiger it is; to take Emerson's admonition as a trumpet call and *"always do what you are afraid to do."*

✳

> *You carry*
> *All the ingredients*
> *To turn your life into a nightmare—*
> *Don't mix them!*
>
> . . . . . .
>
> *You carry all the ingredients*
> *To turn existence into joy,*
> *Mix them, mix*
> *Them!*
>
> —HAFIZ

Is it really that simple? Can we really identify the ingredients to happiness, to a meaningful life, and in a larger sense, to *how things work*, like a family recipe to be mixed? The indisputable answer is, *yes*. Embracing play; fostering close relationships through family, friendships, and community; focusing on the intrinsic, what's on the inside, where the kingdom of heaven resides, rather than on the external markers of power, prestige, or material wealth; serving a purpose greater than ourselves; all of these principles, when regularly put into practice—and it is a practice!—lead to a deeper experience of our most valued emotion, *happiness*. Why? *Because these principles, these behaviors and traits, reflect perfectly how we operate.* When we foster close relationships we become happier because we are hardwired for love and connection; when we serve others we find meaning because we are programmed for compassion and cooperation; when we take time to play and explore the natural world, we become happier because we get in touch with all that is in us and around us, none of which is separate from us.

In the end, happiness is not a concept to be debated, but an experience to be lived. As always, Rumi offers sage advice:

> *Today, like every other day, we wake up empty*
> *and frightened. Don't open the door to the study*
> *and begin reading. Take down a musical instrument.*
> *Let the beauty we love be what we do.*
> *There are hundreds of ways to kneel and kiss the ground.*

Hundreds of ways. Your way, my way, his way, her way—each authentic, each a prayer. So what are you waiting for? Go now. Pick up a musical instrument, play your note, pucker up and kiss the ground. Here's to mud-covered lips, hands swollen from drumming, and feet worn out from dancing. After all, your happiness, my happiness—and since everything is connected, the world's happiness, too!—may very well depend on it.

Dialogue Twenty-five:

FEAR: How can you speak of happiness when you would have people invite sorrow, sadness, and pain?
TRUTH: I would have people understand sorrow, sadness, and pain.

FEAR: You hide behind words. What you offer still hurts them.
TRUTH: And what hurts them, blesses them.

FEAR: Now you are quoting again.
TRUTH: Actually, Hafiz was quoting me.

FEAR: Well, you can quote me, now: I offer a life with less pain.
TRUTH: In the short run.

FEAR: Oh, now who's looking to the future. I thought we weren't supposed to worry about tomorrow!
TRUTH: This is not a worry. It's a fact.

FEAR: That people will suffer in the long run?
TRUTH: They will suffer the knowledge that they did not live their own story.

FEAR: So? Is that so terrible?
TRUTH: It is worse. It is blasphemy.

FEAR: Blasphemy? You exaggerate.
TRUTH: A person's true voice and God's voice are one. To deny your own voice, is to deny God.

FEAR: Are you saying everyone is God?
TRUTH: When you serve God completely, with all you are, His will and your own become the same.

FEAR: You confuse me. What do you want from people?
TRUTH: Everything.

FEAR: A slave master asks for less!
TRUTH: A slave master binds; I set people free.

FEAR: From what?
TRUTH: You.

WHO ARE YOU?

✳

We are already one. But we imagine that we are not.
And what we have to recover is our original unity.
What we have to be is what we are.

—THOMAS MERTON

FOR MUCH OF OUR HISTORY, science believed, and wrongly so, that we could bleed a patient to health. Bloodletting, as the procedure is called, was the intentional withdrawal of blood to prevent or cure disease. But after hundreds of years of this detrimental practice, the procedure suddenly died out. Why? What makes a daily procedure once essential, instantly obsolete? What makes *"one generation abandon the enterprises of another like stranded vessels"*? The answer is all too simple: *the discovery that something does not work,* that a practice, like bloodletting, does not produce a desired result.

And when we stop to consider the principles on which we have built our society—separation; competition; that we are aggressive and selfish, flawed in our nature—do we not reach the same conclusion? Do we not realize that the present-day bloodletting does not work? If what science is now discovering, and what the mystics have told us for millennia is true—that all things are one—do we not see that in our attempts to conquer nature and each other, we are bleeding ourselves, not to health, but to death?

The question that began this exploration—*does an operating manual for life exist, and what is written inside?*—can now be answered. Evidence abounds with recent scientific discoveries of the entanglement of particles, of an energy field that connects all things, of human physiology strengthened by positive states, of cooperation as the ruling order in nature. More evidence is found in the edicts of the saints and sages, all pointing to unity, to oneness as the deepest reality of life. We can no longer dismiss these moral leaders as idealists. With science and spirituality now speaking as one, we arrive at a new understanding; our moral leaders were not idealists, but realists. *"The great moral teachers of humanity were, in a way, artistic geniuses in the art of living,"* Einstein said. What caught the attention of the leading scientist of the 20th century? What is it these geniuses knew? At the core of the teachings of all mystical traditions—whether indigenous, Christian, Jewish, Buddhist, Hindu, or Sufism— is one simple, consistent principle: *love.* And not love as pure sentiment, but *love as practical.* For when we examine how things work, is it not love we find at the center? Love is the root of compassion, which renews human cell structure; love is the foundation of community, which gives our lives meaning and purpose; love is the basis of cooperation, which has enabled our species to survive; love is Desmond Tutu's *"instructions on the box."* Life's Operating Manual might be better labeled *Life's Cooperating Manual,* for what is written inside. Only this: *love is how things work.*

"The power of love, as the basis of the state, has never been tried," said Emerson. It's true, we have yet to make love our societal mandate; is it any surprise we suffer the consequences—a broken

economy, a battered educational system, waning happiness? The compensations of the universe are precise and exacting; put out hate and hate boomerangs back; live in anger and you will not live long; steal from your neighbor and you steal from yourself. As long as we continue to behave outside the way things work, we will further the madness of the present-day world. And it is a kind of madness—this world of *Eat, Pray, Shove*—where we love our neighbor on Sunday and crush him to bits on Monday. It is a sin, this behavior, but not in the traditional sense, as a breach of religious law. Author Whitley Strieber encountered a wise stranger who defined sin this way: *"Sin is denial of the right to thrive."* This is the sin of our day: living in anger, greed, envy, and pride, denying others, ourselves, and all of life the right to thrive. In so doing, we act outside the imperative of life's operating manual. To elevate competition and disproportionately reward the winners, to take more than we need, to deny connection as life's primary reality, to see ourselves as separate from one another and nature, is to continue our bloodletting ways. Is it not time we tell a different story, a new story, *the story of connection and cooperation, the story that love is how things work?*

And so we have come full circle, and return to the essential question: *who are you?* From a scientific perspective, you are miraculous. You are stardust. You contain the same energy and matter that created the universe 13 billion years ago. You were once that energy—inside the infinitesimally small point of light that began all of life. Everything around you, everything you can see, touch, and taste, is made of this matter, this same universal energy: the water that shines, the tree that reaches, the bird in flight, the grass that grows. The saints and sages across the ages said it this way: *you are brothers and sisters with all of creation.* If who you are and how things work are one and the same, then who you are is love.

There is a famous parable about a man who lived in a cottage by the sea. Every morning, the man went fishing and caught just enough fish for the day. Afterward, he would spend time playing with his son, take a siesta, and enjoy lunch with his family. In the evening, he and his wife would meet friends at a local bar, where they would tell stories, play music, and dance the night away. One day, a tourist saw the fisherman and his meager catch and asked, *"Why do you only catch three or four fish?" "That is all my family needs for today,"* the fisherman replied. But the tourist had gone to business school and could not help but offer advice: *"You know, if you catch a few more fish and sell them at the market, you could make some extra money." "Why would I want to do that?"* the fisherman asked. *"With the extra money you could save up and buy a boat. Then, you could catch even more fish, and make even more money, which you could use to buy an entire fleet of boats!" "Why would I need so many boats?"* queried the fisherman. *"Don't you see? With a fleet of boats, you could sell more fish, and with the extra money, you could move to New York, run an international business and sell fish all over the world!" "And how long would this take?"* the fisherman asked. *"Maybe 10 or 20 years,"* the businessman said. *"Then what?"* the fisherman said. *"Then you could sell your company for millions, retire, buy a cottage by the sea, go fishing every morning, take a siesta every afternoon, enjoy lunch with your family, and spend the evenings with friends, playing music and dancing!"*

How many of us today are like this businessman, blindly chasing what has been in front of us all along? What will it take for us to realize what we are looking for and the looker are one and the same? As Rumi said, "*I have lived on the lip of insanity, wanting to know reasons, knocking on a door. It opens. I've been knocking from the inside!*"

✴

I wish I could show you,
When you are lonely or in darkness,
The Astonishing Light
Of your own Being.

With these four ecstatic lines, Hafiz offers us his answer to our question; *the very light of your being is astonishing!* Thomas Merton echoes Hafiz when he writes:

As if the sorrows and stupidities of the human condition could overwhelm me, now that I realize what we all are. And if only everybody could realize this! But it cannot be explained. There is no way of telling people that they are all walking around shining like the sun.

Merton goes one step further with this insight:

Finally I am coming to the conclusion that my highest ambition is to be what I already am.

Wait a minute. What about worldly status, money, success, and power? Merton saw through all of that, and he invites us to do the same. Can you imagine? What a lesson to embrace, to embody, and even to teach. To declare to our kids that they don't have to *be* someone, they already *are* someone.

You see (and it is a matter of sight!), what we are telling ourselves, the command to succeed and be someone, is just a story; it's a story based on expectations. It's temporal and finite. It is not who you really are. The Sufi mystic, Meera, offers this insight: *to play your role in time, you must know who you are in eternity.* And who you are is God among us in one of His myriad disguises. You're not just a drop in the ocean; you're the entire ocean in a drop. So take a look in the mirror. What you see staring back is the answer, the solution to the world's problems. Nothing need be invented, no great leader need come. You are it. Each step taken in love, heals. Each act of kindness sends a ripple effect outward. No act is too small. No gesture insignificant. The truth is, we are not powerless, but infinitely powerful. And what is this power? It is the power to love. It is your birthright. It is who you are and have always been. It is how things work. May you be blessed with the knowing that dissolves the knower; may you unlock the heart's secret and carry it forth: that all is connected; that all is one; that all is God in drag. To that end . . .

Dialogue Twenty-six:

FEAR: So that's it? Your book is surprisingly simple.

TRUTH: As I said, there is nothing new here.

FEAR: And you do not feel the slightest bit remorseful or even irresponsible?
TRUTH: Irresponsible? Why?

FEAR: Because you are giving people false hope.
TRUTH: False hope is not what I wish to give people. Or any hope, for that matter.

FEAR: You don't wish to give people hope? Your entire book is about hope!
TRUTH: Hope is the desire for something to be so, for some result to occur. Truth does not need results, and therefore does not need hope; truth rests in the knowledge of what already is.

FEAR: So now it is wrong for people to hope? Would you not have them hope for a better tomorrow?
TRUTH: I would have them know that a better tomorrow comes when the truth of today is fully known and fully lived.

FEAR: But Democrats *hope* Republicans will come around and vice versa. What's wrong with that?
TRUTH: It is not wrong; it is inefficient. Live your truth in openness, in humility. Share it with all. Those who are meant to come around will come around.

FEAR: I don't understand you. You offer no practical advice. What is the reader supposed to do?
TRUTH: This book is not about what to do, but about who to be. From there all doing will emanate.

FEAR: That's a cop-out.

TRUTH: Then Jesus was a cop-out. He did not offer a six-step program or ten healthy habits. He taught love. He lived love. He was love. How that love manifests in an individual's life is up to that individual.

FEAR: People want something practical! Or is it that you have nothing practical to offer?

TRUTH: People know what they need to do. The question is, what is keeping them from doing it?

FEAR: And you will say it is me.

TRUTH: Fear, you see everything as your enemy. It is not so. The other is not your enemy. Neither is suffering. Nor pain. And least of all, me.

FEAR: You are not my enemy? Ha! I know how you feel about me!

TRUTH: I feel a lot of things. Mostly gratitude.

FEAR: You are grateful for me? Since when?

TRUTH: You are an instructor, Fear. Where you appear, there is rottenness. Wrongs that must be righted.

FEAR: This is not gratitude. This is blame!

TRUTH: Is it blame to say that without you, I would not have known in what direction I needed to go? All these years, by telling me what *not* to do, you have told me precisely what *to* do. So, yes, Fear. Even for you, I am thankful.

(A long pause.)

FEAR: I don't like it when you do that.
TRUTH: Do what?

FEAR: Show appreciation. It makes me feel . . . weak.

(ANOTHER long pause.)

FEAR: And stop looking at me. You know what that does to me.

(Truth continues, looks right into Fear. And then, barely audible . . .)

FEAR: I don't feel like talking anymore.
TRUTH: I understand.

FEAR: I am not going away, you know? You will hear from me again. The next time things don't go as planned. Or there's a disappointment.
TRUTH: I'm counting on it. How else would I know what *not* to do?

EPILOGUE

✳

The mind, this globe of awareness,
is a starry universe that
when you push off from it with your foot,
a thousand new roads come clear.

—RUMI

What saves a man is to take a step. Then another step.

—ANTOINE DE SAINT-EXUPÉRY

IT'S POSSIBLE, IF YOU'RE THIS FAR ALONG IN THE BOOK, that your worldview, if not completely shattered, has at least been called into question. I can relate. Some ten years ago, after reading *Ishmael*, that paradigm-bashing book recommended by God himself, Morgan Freeman, I raced back and anxiously posed this question: *"Okay, Morgan, I get it. My view of the world is now officially upside down. What the heck do I do? What do any of us do?"* I'll never forget what he told me. The strongest, wisest man I knew, looked at me squarely and said, *"I have no idea, son."* *"What?!"* I screamed inside. *"You can't just leave me here. Tell me something to do! Anything!"* But he didn't. He just left me, on my own, walking—no, staggering—into a world gone wrong, into a world I somehow had to rethink my place in.

It has never been the intention of this book to leave you feeling bad, but to help you feel what is. There is an enormous difference. If, God forbid, you discover tomorrow you have skin cancer, would you judge yourself? I hope not. You would likely, immediately, set out on a course to rid yourself of that cancer. Self-criticism would be of little value. The skin cancer just is. That's how I hope each of us can view our own participation in a world infected with a cancerous ideology. It does little good to judge it. Simply see it, recognize the cancer, and set out on a course, little by little, step by step, to purge your own participation in that cancer as best you can.

Here's the good news: I am now eternally grateful for Morgan's lack of direction, for his nonanswer. Why? Because the path I have taken over the past 10 years is not his, but my own. Just as the path you will take now must be your own. You can only love the world in the context of loving yourself. Be patient with your walk. It's taken me time, some 10 to 15 years, to get where I am presently standing. And I am still very much a work in progress. Peace Pilgrim, a modern-day saint, experienced a similar timeline; she said it took her *15 years from the knowing to the doing.* Give yourself that time. Without judgment. Expend little effort "shoulding" on yourself, and more in *seeing* yourself, and freeing yourself from fear and the expectations of others.

I make you this promise: even the slightest change can have an infinite impact—a conversation had, a courageous question asked, a kind act offered—each begins the domino effect: one domino felling another, a butterfly's wing flapping here, a spark igniting there. This, I believe, is what faith is—knowing that following your own heart plants seeds in fields beyond your awareness. And though you may never see those seeds blossom, trust that they will indeed blossom and bear fruit in the souls of men you may never meet. And so, as you question, as you change, as your own *shift* hits the fan, recall the insight of the mystic, the visionary prophet, Julian of Norwich, who assures us with the certainty of one who has glimpsed the godhead:

"All shall be well, and all shall be well, and all manner of things shall be well."

ENDNOTES

THE WORLD IS BROKEN

What will ambition do: Mary Oliver, "Am I Not Among the Early Risers" in *West Wind* (Houghton Mifflin, New York: 1998).

THE CRISIS OF OUR TIME

In spite of these spectacular strides: Martin Luther King, Jr., 1964 Nobel Prize acceptance speech, http://www.nobelprize.org/nobel_prizes/peace /laureates/1964/king-lecture.html.

LIFE'S OPERATING MANUAL

What have I ever lost: Jalal al-Din Rumi, translated by Coleman Barks, *The Essential Rumi* (HarperCollins, New York: 2004).

Death is a doorway: Mary Oliver, "Have You Ever Tried to Enter the Long Black Branches" in *West Wind* (Houghton Mifflin, New York: 1998).

TWO MASTERS

I don't think there is such a thing: Kabir, translated by Daniel Ladinsky, "An Intelligent Rich Person" in *Love Poems from God* (Penguin, New York: 2002).

INCEPTION

No one lives his life: Rainer Maria Rilke, translated by Anita Barrows and Jo-anna Macy, *Rilke's Book of Hours* (Berkley Publishing Group, New York: 2005).

To be full: Psalm 46:10.

And where is the power: Thomas Merton, *Raids on the Unspeakable* (New Directions, New York: 1966).

Almost one is four: Amy Goldstein, "Hunger a growing problem in America, USDA reports," *The Washington Post,* November 17, 2009: http://www.washingtonpost.com/wp-dyn/content/article/2009/11/16/AR2009111601598.html.

Fifty percent of our college: Mental Health on MSNBC, reported by Alex Johnson, "Half of College Students Consider Suicide," August 18, 2008: http://www.msnbc.msn.com/id/26272639/ns/health-mental_health/t/half-college-students-consider-suicide/.

DIVIDING GOD

We have exhausted ourselves: Hafiz, translated by Daniel Ladinsky, "Dividing God" in *The Gift* (Compass, New York: 1999).

THE INDIGENOUS STORY

The President in Washington: Brain Swann and Arnold Krupat, eds., *Recovering the Word* (University of California Press, Berkeley: 1987).

THE TYRANNY OF AGRICULTURE

That mankind can now produce: Daniel Quinn in *Ishmael* (Bantam Books, New York: 1995), *My Ishmael* (Bantam Books, New York: 1998), and *The Story of B* (Bantam Books, New York: 1997).

SPOOKY ACTION

Spooky action at a distance: Brian Greene, "Spooky Action at a Distance," *Nova,* September 22, 2011: http://www.pbs.org/wgbh/nova/physics/spooky-action-distance.html.

Double slit experiment: Edwin Cartlidge, "New 'Double Slit' Experiment Skirts Uncertainty Principle," *Scientific American,* June 2, 2011: http://www.scientificamerican.com/article.cfm?id=new-double-slit-experiment-skirts-uncertainty-principle.

When does your dog know: Rupert Sheldrake, *Dogs that Know When Their Owners are Coming Home* (Three Rivers Press, New York: 2011).

Tied in a single garment: Martin Luther King, Jr., "Letter from a Birmingham Jail," April 16, 1963.

THE SCIENCE OF LOVE

Admit Somthing: Hafiz, translated by Daniel Ladinsky, "Admit something" in *Love Poems from God* (Penguin, New York: 2002).

The Empathic Civilization: Jeremy Rifkin, *The Empathic Civilization* (Penguin, New York: 2009).

Evolutionary biologist Elisabet Sahtouris: http://www.sahtouris.com.

In 1976, a study: Abraham Sagi and Martin Hoffman, "Empathetic Distress in the Newborn," *Developmental Psychology* 12, no. 2 (March 1976): 175–76.

There's a power in me: Rainer Maria Rilke, translated by Anita Barrows and Joanna Macy, "Da neigt sich die Stunde und rührt mich an" in *Rilke's Book of Hours* (Berkley Publishing Group, New York: 2005).

Without me all shape: Hafiz, translated by Daniel Ladinsky, *A Year with Hafiz* (Penguin, New York: 2006).

ECONO-ME

We have a greed: Recorded by Eddie Vedder, "Society," *Into the Wild,* (J. Records: 2012), original lyrics by Jerry Hannan.

It is difficult to get a man: Upton Sinclair, *I, Candidate for Governor* (University of California Press, Berkeley: 1935).

The sun is but a morning star: Henry David Thoreau, *Walden* (Thomas Y. Crowell & Co., New York: 1910).

LAWS THAT ARE NOT LAWS

34.4 trillion dollars: Henry CK Liu, "The Crisis of Wealth Destruction," *Asia Times,* April 13, 2010: http://atimes.com/atimes/Global_Economy/LD13Dj05.html.

In this country alone: Amy Goldstein, "Hunger a growing problem in America, USDA reports," *The Washington Post,* November 17, 2009: http://www.washingtonpost.com/wp-dyn/content/article/2009/11/16/AR2009111601598.html.

1 percent of the population: James Randerson, "World's richest 1% own 40% of all wealth, UN report discovers," *The Guardian,* December 6, 2006: http://www.guardian.co.uk/money/2006/dec/06/business.internationalnews.

One billion people: "Fast Fact: The Faces of Poverty," *Millennium Project* (2006): http://www.unmillenniumproject.org/resources/fastfacts_e.htm.

Just like stopping at a traffic light: Thom Hartmann, *The Last Hours of Ancient Sunlight* (Three Rivers Press, New York: 2004).

GROWTH IS GOOD

Here's a deeply disturbing statistic: Jeremy Rifkin, *The Empathic Civilization* (Penguin, New York: 2009).

If all the insects were to disappear: Jonas Salk, as quoted by Ken Robinson, "Ken Robinson says schools kill creativity," TED, June 2006: http://www.ted .com/talks/ken_robinson_says_schools_kill_creativity.html.

It is easier for a camel: Matthew 19:24.

Do not store up: Mathew 6:19.

The problem is, a prayer: Ralph Waldo Emerson, "Self-Reliance" in *Selected Writings of Ralph Waldo Emerson* (Penguin, New York: 2011).

A hole in a flute: Hafiz, translated by Daniel Ladinsky, "A Hole in a Flute" in *The Gift* (Compass, New York: 1999).

ALRIGHTY THEN!

Why go to sleep: Hafiz, translated by Daniel Ladinsky, "Of Course Things Like That Can Happen" in *I Heard God Laughing* (Penguin, New York: 2006).

THE LION AND THE GAZELLE

You give but little: Kahlil Gibran, "On Giving" in *The Prophet* (Oneworld, Oxford, England: 1998).

TWENTY-FOUR DOLLARS

Let me say this before rain: Thomas Merton, *Raids on the Unspeakable* (New Directions, New York: 1966).

Now art glorifies the artist: Thomas Klise, *The Last Western* (Argus Communications, Niles, IL: 1974).

Men of an extraordinary success: Ralph Waldo Emerson, "Spiritual Laws" in *The Spiritual Emerson* (Penguin, New York: 2008).

Nor do I believe: Wendell Berry, "Some Further Words" in *The Mad Farmer Poems* (Counterpoint, Berkeley, CA: 2008).

"Intellectual property" names the deed: Wendell Berry, "Some Further Words" in *The Mad Farmer Poems* (Counterpoint, Berkeley, CA: 2008).

Who owns the patent: George Johnson, "Once Again, a Man with a Mission," *The New York Times,* November 25, 1990: http://www
.nytimes.com/1990/11/25/magazine/once-again-a-man-with-a-mission
.html?pagewanted=all.

The organs would starve: Elisabet Sahtouris, "The Biology of Globalization," *Perspectives on Business and Global Change,* September 1997.

The heart and soul of all men: Ralph Waldo Emerson, "Compensation" in *The Portable Emerson* (Penguin, New York: 1981).

THE RICHEST MAN IN TOWN

The best way to find yourself: This quote is commonly attributed to Mahatma Gandhi.

Men such as they are: Ralph Waldo Emerson, "The American Scholar" in *The Portable Emerson* (Penguin, New York: 1981).

Be still, and know: Psalm 46:10.

EDUCA-SHUN

Omnipresence is not just a rumor: Hafiz, translated by Daniel Ladinsky, *A Year with Hafiz* (Penguin, New York: 2006).

I can never be what I ought to be: Martin Luther King, Jr., "Remaining Awake Through a Great Revolution," commencement address at Oberlin College, June 1965: http://www.oberlin.edu/external/EOG/BlackHistoryMonth
/MLK/CommAddress.html.

To promote student achievement: U.S. Department of Education mission statement, http://www2.ed.gov/about/landing.jhtml.

The basic thing nobody asks: John Lennon as quoted in *The Columbia Dictionary of Quotations,* Robert Andrews, ed. (Columbia University Press, New York: 1993).

A recent MSNBC report: Mental Health on MSNBC, reported by Alex Johnson, "Half of College Students Consider Suicide," August 18, 2008: http://www.msnbc.msn.com/id/26272639/ns/health-mental_health/t/half-college-students-consider-suicide/.

If I saw a competitor drowning: Ray Kroc as quoted in "Polishing the Golden Arches," Dyan Machan, *Forbes,* June 15, 1998: http://www.forbes.com/global/1998/0615/0106024a.html.

Plunder taken from an enemy: Merriam-Webster's Collegiate Dictionary, Eleventh Edition.

He who has a thousand friends: Ali ibn-Abi-Talib as quoted in *Bartlett's Familiar Quotations, Seventeenth Edition,* John Bartlett (Little, Brown and Company, New York: 2002).

THE GOSPEL OF THOMAS

I was a fish: George Reavis, *The Animal School* (Crystal Springs, Peterborough, NH: 1999).

To me education is a leading out: Muriel Spark, *The Prime of Miss Jean Brodie* (HarperCollins, New York: 1999).

At the age of five: Finley Eversole as quoted in *Walking on Water,* Madeleine L'Engle (North Point Press, New York: 1995).

We are turning our children: Personal conversation.

7000 students drop out of school every day: CNN Newsroom, Transcript, "Education Reform Road Trip/School Challenges in California," Tony Harris, August 30, 2010: http://edition.cnn.com/TRANSCRIPTS/1008/30/cnr.04.html.

Even Albert Einstein: James Pressley, "Buffet, McCartney Have It, Most of Us Don't; No, Not Money," *Bloomberg,* February 9, 2009: http://www.bloomberg.com/apps/news?pid=newsarchive&sid=aeSSU3dV0I78&refer=m.

Florida's latest vow: Eric Kelderman, "Governor Says Florida has Enough Anthropologists, Calls for Spending on Job-Producing Fields," *The Chronicle of Higher Education,* October 11, 2011: http://chronicle.com/blogs/ticker/florida-governor-favors-more-state-money-for-math-and-science-degrees/37144.

Georgia schools now intend: Nancy Badertscher, "Georgia to Require Students to Pick Career Path," *The Atlanta Journal-Constitution*, December 12, 2011: http://www.ajc.com/news/news/local/georgia-to-require-students-to-pick-career-path/nQPRN.

For Occupation: Emily Dickinson, "I Dwell in Possibility" in *The Poems of Emily Dickinson*, R.W. Franklin, ed. (Harvard University Press, Cambridge, MA: 1998).

GENTLE CONTEMPT

When I was 5 years old: Commonly attributed to John Lennon.

Without a gentle contempt: G.K. Chesterton, *G.K. Chesterton, Collected Works: The Illustrated London News: 1929–1931* (Ignatius Press, San Francisco, CA: 1992).

God, disguised as myriad things: Hafiz, translated by Daniel Ladinsky, "You're It" in *The Gift* (Compass, New York: 1999).

SCHADENFREUDE

The least of the work: Thomas Merton, "Learning to Live" in *Love and Living* (Farrar, Straus, and Giroux, New York: 1979).

Preach the gospel: Commonly attributed to St. Francis.

Every child in America: U.S. Department of Education, *A Blueprint for Reform,* March 2010: http://www2.ed.gov/policy/elsec/leg/blueprint/blueprint.pdf.

HAPPINESS

We can no more halve things: Ralph Waldo Emerson, "Compensation" in *The Portable Emerson* (Penguin, New York: 1981).

All shall be well: Julian of Norwich, *Revelations of Divine Love* (Dover Publications, Mineola, NY: 2006).

The rose celebrates: Coleman Barks quoting Rumi in the documentary *I AM*.

When an archer shoots: Thomas Merton, "The Need to Win" in *The Way of Chuang Tzu* (Shambhala Publications, Boston, MA: 2004).

The highest price: Ralph Waldo Emerson, "Compensation" in *The Portable Emerson* (Penguin, New York: 1981).

SHOW ME THE MONEY!

74 percent of our youth: Madeleine L'Engle, *Walking on Water* (North Point Press, New York: 1995).

You want the first elements: Thomas Merton, "Keng's Disciple" in *The Way of Chuang Tzu* (Shambhala Publications, Boston, MA: 2004).

Unless ye become like these little children: Matthew 18:3.

Thank you, Father, for hiding these things: Matthew 11:25.

LITTLE TOMMY SHADYAC

What is serious to men is often very trivial: Thomas Merton, "The Contemplative Dance" in *On Christian Contemplation* (New Directions, New York: 2012).

Unless you leave mother: Matthew 10:37.

Always do what you are afraid to do: Ralph Waldo Emerson, "Heroism" in *The Essays of Ralph Waldo Emerson* (Harvard University Press, Cambridge, MA: 1987).

You carry all the ingredients: Hafiz, translated by Daniel Ladinsky, "To Build a Swing" in *The Gift* (Compass, New York: 1999).

Today, like every other day: Rumi, translated by Coleman Barks, "Today, like every other day, we wake up empty" in *Rumi: The Book of Love* (HarperCollins, New York: 2005).

WHO ARE YOU?

One generation abandons the enterprises: Henry David Thoreau, *Walden* (Thomas Y. Crowell & Co., New York: 1910).

The great moral teachers: Albert Einstein, "Religion and Science: Irreconcilable?" in *Ideas and Opinions* (Broadway, New York: 1995).

The power of love, as the basis of the state: Ralph Waldo Emerson, *The Tao of Emerson* (Modern Library, New York: 2007).

Sin is denial: Whitley Strieber quoted in "Whitley Strieber, 'Communion'" Author, Describes Bizarre Encounter with Mystery Man," Lee Speigel, *The Huffington Post,* November 7, 2011: http://www.huffingtonpost.com/2011/09/07/communion-author-whitley-strieber_n_943681.html.

I have lived on the lip of insanity: Rumi, translated by Coleman Barks, "I have lived on the lip . . ." in *The Essential Rumi* (HarperCollins, New York: 1995).

I wish I could show you: Hafiz, translated by Daniel Ladinsky, *I Heard God Laughing* (Penguin, New York: 2006).

As if the sorrows and stupidities: Thomas Merton, "Shining Like the Sun" in *A Year with Thomas Merton* (HarperCollins, New York: 2004).

Finally I am coming: Thomas Merton, "Godlikeness Begins at Home" in *A Year with Thomas Merton* (HarperCollins, New York: 2004).

You're not just a drop: Commonly attributed to Rumi.

The mind, this globe of awareness: Rumi, translated by Coleman Barks, "Any Chance Meeting" in *The Essential Rumi* (HarperCollins, New York: 2001).

PERMISSIONS

TWENTY-FOUR DOLLARS

"Some Further Words" by Wendell Berry. Copyright © 2008 by Wendell Berry from *The Mad Farmer Poems*. Reprinted by permission of the publisher.

THE GOSPEL OF THOMAS

"I Dwell in Possibility" from *The Poems of Emily Dickinson*. Reprinted by permission of the publishers and the Trustees of Amherst College from *The Poems of Emily Dickinson, Reading Edition,* edited by Ralph W. Franklin, Cambridge, Mass.: The Belknap Press of Harvard University Press, Copyright © 1998, 1999 by President and Fellows of Harvard College. Copyright © 1951, 1955, 1979 by the President and Fellows of Harvard College.

GENTLE CONTEMPT

Excerpt from "You're It" by Hafiz, translated by Daniel Ladinsky in *The Gift*. © 1999 Daniel Ladinsky. Used by permission of Daniel Ladinsky.

SHOW ME THE MONEY!

"Keng's Disciple" from *The Way of Chuang Tzu* by Thomas Merton, copyright © 1965 by the Abbey of Gethsemani. Reprinted by permission of New Directions Publishing Corp.

LITTLE TOMMY SHADYAC

Excerpt from "To Build a Swing" by Hafiz, translated by Daniel Ladinsky in *The Gift*. © 1999 Daniel Ladinsky. Used by permission of Daniel Ladinsky.

Excerpt from "Today, like every other day, we wake up empty" by Rumi, translated by Coleman Barks, from *Rumi: The Book of Love*. © 2003 by Coleman Barks. Used by permission of Coleman Barks.

WHO ARE YOU?

Excerpt from "I have lived on the lip" by Rumi, translated by Coleman Barks, from *The Essential Rumi*. © 2004 by Coleman Barks. Used by permission of Coleman Barks.

EPILOGUE

ABOUT THE AUTHOR

TOM SHADYAC is the film director behind such blockbuster hits as *Ace Ventura: Pet Detective; The Nutty Professor; Liar, Liar; Patch Adams;* and *Bruce Almighty.* A recent brush with death compelled Tom to make his latest film, *I AM,* a documentary that asks some of today's most profound thinkers two questions: "What's wrong with the world?" and "What can we do about it?"

We hope you enjoyed this Hay House book. If you'd like to receive our online catalog featuring additional information on Hay House books and products, or if you'd like to find out more about the Hay Foundation, please contact:

Hay House, Inc., P.O. Box 5100, Carlsbad, CA 92018-5100
(760) 431-7695 or (800) 654-5126
(760) 431-6948 (fax) or (800) 650-5115 (fax)
www.hayhouse.com® • **www.hayfoundation.org**

✸

Published and distributed in Australia by: Hay House Australia Pty. Ltd., 18/36 Ralph St., Alexandria NSW 2015 • *Phone:* 612-9669-4299 *Fax:* 612-9669-4144 • www.hayhouse.com.au

Published and distributed in the United Kingdom by: Hay House UK, Ltd., Astley House, 33 Notting Hill Gate, London W11 3JQ *Phone:* 44-20-3675-2450 • *Fax:* 44-20-3675-2451 • www.hayhouse.co.uk

Published and distributed in the Republic of South Africa by: Hay House SA (Pty), Ltd., P.O. Box 990, Witkoppen 2068 *Phone/Fax:* 27-11-467-8904 • www.hayhouse.co.za

Published in India by: Hay House Publishers India, Muskaan Complex, Plot No. 3, B-2, Vasant Kunj, New Delhi 110 070 • *Phone:* 91-11-4176-1620 • *Fax:* 91-11-4176-1630 • www.hayhouse.co.in

Distributed in Canada by: Raincoast, 9050 Shaughnessy St., Vancouver, B.C. V6P 6E5 • *Phone:* (604) 323-7100 *Fax:* (604) 323-2600 • www.raincoast.com

✸

<u>Take Your Soul on a Vacation</u>

Visit **www.HealYourLife.com®** to regroup, recharge, and reconnect with your own magnificence. Featuring blogs, mind-body-spirit news, and life-changing wisdom from Louise Hay and friends.

Visit **www.HealYourLife.com** today!